UNCOVERING Amy

How I Healed My Multiple Personality Disorder and My Painful Journey to True Mental Health

By Amelia South and Bryan Redfield

Certified Herbalist, Reprogramming Coach

Cover Artwork and Design by Gail Nelson

South, Amelia Uncovering Amy

Copyright © 2026 by Black Sun Farm, LLC. and Amelia South

amelia@nobsherbalist.com

Published in the United States of America by Black Sun Publishing

Black Sun Publishing
Danielson, CT 06239

ISBN: 979-8-9944322-3-5

UNCOVERING Amy

How I Healed My Multiple Personality Disorder and My Painful Journey to True Mental Health

By Amelia South and Bryan Redfield

Originators of the Super Team™
Brain Training Method.

Disclaimer

I am not a doctor. I do not have a degree in Psychology. I am an Herbalist with a very interesting story to tell.

Bryan Redfield has an AA in Psychology and studied Psychology at UCLA.

Bryan created this training method to heal his own mental state. I would not be who I am today without his help. This method he developed has helped many people over the years. Maybe now it will help you.

Oxford English Dictionary

cure

/kyoor/

verb

relieve (a person or animal) of the symptoms of a disease or condition.

"he was cured of the disease"

If that's the definition, then I'm using the word correctly, whether I have a PhD or not.

INTRODUCTION

There are three things life has taught me over the last few years of my own transformation:

1) 1. Don't assume you know more today than you will know tomorrow.

2) 2. No one will EVER love you exactly in the perfect way or exactly the way you want them to the same way that you are capable of loving yourself.

3) 3. Dissociative Identity Disorder (formerly called Multiple Personality Disorder) is a greatly misunderstood and misdiagnosed problem that can be resolved with the method I used.

Before you come after me with torches and pitchforks, I suggest you read this book. It might alter your perspective.

For the first time in my life, I have true mental health. I can look back at old photos of me or think of memories and see my own dysfunction staring me in the face.

I can look at most people and within 5 minutes of talking with them see their dysfunctions too. It's okay, most people are messed up. You can blame your parents and generations upon generations of messed up people messing up their kids.

Few people escape this cycle. I'm grateful to be one of the few.

I'm not saying that egotistically or in a holier-than-thou way. Millions upon millions of people are in therapy every day to deal with their dysfunction. Hundreds of thousands of people choose to become therapists to help people through their problems. Most therapists don't know what the hell they're doing or can only give you some token relief. But most people aren't actually open to resolving their problems.

Most people want a band-aid. A quick fix. Something to take the edge off, so they can go on living their generally unsatisfying lives with a short break now and then given either by drugs or a decent therapist helping them feel better for a day or so. Then their problems return and they're back to square one, talking with the therapist again, wondering why it's taking so long to resolve their issues.

It's because they aren't resolving anything. They're just talking about it.

If you've been seeing the same therapist for more than three years and you still don't feel any better about your life or yourself, your therapist sucks. It does not take that long to solve your problems.

Here's the thing: if you're in enough pain, you will do ANYTHING to fix the problem. To prove my point:

Say you have to poop really bad, like you can feel diarrhea coming and there's no way to stop it. Do you care about someone telling you that your problems are all in your head or that you should have eaten something different or if you eat this vitamin, it will make you feel better in a few hours? Or do you listen to the one person who tells you, "the toilet's right over there!"

I'm telling you that I know where the toilet is.

It's up to you to decide if you'd rather just try to hold it in and deal with the discomfort or just shit and get over it completely.

What follows is the story of what happened to me to learn all this. *I've changed most of the names of people and places, but the events are all true.* I do not care whether you believe me or not. I have felt compelled to tell this story for some time now and I'm writing it down before the details get too fuzzy.

You are reading this book because you were meant to. The Universe put it into your hands. There are no mistakes.

Most of the people who read this book will not understand it. I don't care if you're a psychiatrist or a psychologist with 40 years of clinical experience under your belt. You're going to think I'm full of shit or don't know what I'm talking about because I haven't got the same PhD you do and there's no way some random person without the same degree as you could possibly know the answer to this problem.

In my experience, professionals get into psychology for one of two reasons: either they want to understand their own mental health problems, or they desperately want to feel superior to everyone around them. I'm sure most of them also want to help people, but you can't help someone through something you don't understand. I don't care what your motivation was for going into your profession, I can promise you that until you have LIVED this, you will never understand it.

You don't have to understand it, but the person who needs this solution will hear me out.

I hope my story helps someone ... I'm pretty sure it will.

Important notes: I am a white woman, pagan for well over 25 years (though I honestly don't associate myself with any particular religious structure anymore now). Much of this book involves Native American / American Indian / Indigenous culture and references. I want you to know that I love, respect, admire, and appreciate Native culture here in America and I do my best to practice what they teach, despite not having been raised as part of their culture in this lifetime.

During the events of this book, I was in a period of my life where I was sincerely hoping to be a Native American or be adopted into their culture somehow. I am not a professional historian or an expert on their culture, but I do have some experience with it in research not mentioned in this book. If I get any details or terms wrong in this book, it is accidental, and I sincerely apologize.

Final note: I had never heard of IFS (Internal Family Systems) until after I wrote the first draft of this book and a psychologist friend told me that this was similar. This book has absolutely nothing to do with IFS. It's interesting to me that both Bryan and Dick Schwartz came up with similar healing methodologies in the 1980s.

After exploring how both methods work, I can honestly say I prefer Super Team training.

You can decide for yourself.

Preface

The abuse you suffered as a child was no less damaging whether it was emotional, physical, mental, sexual, or even spiritual.

Nobody's parents set out to raise a fucked-up kid. It just happens, because they know no other way … they have no choice but to follow their own programming that they got from the people who raised them.

Their father was a bully to them when they were being raised, so they are, in turn, forceful in bending you to their will. Their mother manipulated them with tears and guilt to get her way, so yours uses the same tactics on you.

It's a vicious, repetitive cycle that each generation tries to escape. But few manage it.

You can end the cycle. You have the power to change your program. No matter what happened to you during your formative years, no matter how badly you were beaten up, YOU can get your mental health back.

You can take control back, even when it seems all hope is lost.

I'm starting at my beginning for context. Your story may be completely different from mine, but the underlying truth is the same: your earliest experiences in life shaped everything about who you are right now. Everything you believe about the world around you and how it works, everything you think you owe someone or that they owe you, every reaction you have to any circumstance, it was all programmed into you from the day you were born through about age six.

Everything you believe about your own life right now is going to be challenged. You doubt your own senses, you think you may be insane, but in truth, you picked up this story for a reason.

You're not broken. You're not crazy.

And you're not alone.

Backstory (Cliff's Notes Version)

I was born in 1983, the first of two daughters that my parents' loveless marriage produced. They were divorced by the time I was 5, and shortly after my mother started dating a man who owned a local business. Although they never married, they were together until his death a couple of years ago. My father remarried when I was 6 but then divorced my first stepmother in favor of another woman when I was 15. Mom got primary custody when I was 5 and we would visit Dad every other weekend.

Mom worked full time, so my sister and I spent much of my childhood at various babysitters and schools When we were young she and my stepfather took us RV camping regularly all over New England and a few times down to Florida. He and his family determined everything I knew about what it was like to be wealthy. And they were all terrible people, scamming their friends and customers, loan sharking, bribing cops, and more.

From the youngest age I couldn't stand my stepfather. He was a raging alcoholic, starting each day with a mug of coffee and a Budweiser. He didn't care at all about personal space. He would throw a cup of cold water at me in the morning to wake me up for school or sometimes when I was in the shower (before I hit puberty) just for the fun of hearing me scream. He would push one of my fingers down into my hand until I cried and got down on my knees in pain and wouldn't stop until after I had given him a kiss on the cheek. He made it known that women were sex objects as soon as they hit puberty.

At age 11 I chose to move in with my father (and visit my mom on the weekends) so that I could escape my stepfather. I changed school systems, going from Catholic school for the previous 3 years into a public school. My sister and I were never really close after I moved out.

I recall being 16 at my mom's house and coming downstairs for breakfast one morning, when my stepfather looked at me from the kitchen and told me that my breasts looked nice that day. I told him that was sexual harassment and I could call the police on him. He got pissed off and walked away in a huff. I got yelled at by my mother, she said we were living in HIS house, and he was paying most of the bills, so he could treat me however he wanted.

My stepmother, while not physically abusive, swore like a sailor and hoarded animals as well as plants. Every windowsill was full of plants, there were three bird cages with parakeets in the kitchen, three dogs, nine cats, and various hamsters, fish tanks, and hermit crabs over the years. She and my dad worked full time as well but did not make half as much as my stepfather, so although they bought a nice house in rural Connecticut for us to grow up in, we never felt like we had the money to go fun places or do fun things. Instead, we spent many weekends digging in and planting her gardens or going hiking at nearby trails. I loved playing in the woods, and I was eventually given my own wristwatch so that Dad could say "be home by 4" and just send me off (with a quarter for an emergency call) to do whatever I wanted for the day. The 90s were great.

Both of the main male role models in my life treated women as if their only worth was to be sexual satisfaction for their man and to give him children. When I hit puberty and suddenly had large breasts, my mother gleefully exploited them whenever she could (hers were small) and dressed me in whatever shirts or dresses would show off my great rack to whatever man wanted to look. I knew that my worth as a woman was tied to my ability to give pleasure to men and that my breasts were the best thing about me. All the kids at school had told me I was ugly and my father certainly made me feel ugly for years, so I had the self-esteem of a naked mole rat.

I got my first boyfriend when I was 17 and lost my virginity not much after. I was very controlling in that relationship. It lasted over three years and I nearly married him. At age 20, I had a personal epiphany that he was NOT the only man in the world who would ever find me attractive and so I left him and started dating other men. I used my body as a tool to reel them in, and I made sure that I was "the cool nerd girl" who liked all the same things they liked. I started dating sailors from the local naval base because I had more confidence around men who didn't see women very often.

I had decided to renounce Catholicism at age 12 and chose to follow pagan beliefs around age 15. I started dabbling in herbalism and would continue my love of working with plants, nature, and studying indigenous practices for many years. This is relevant.

In 2006, I moved clear across the country from Connecticut to Washington State to live with a boyfriend in the Navy who'd been stationed there. I eventually met another sailor at a party whom I ended up deciding to marry a year later, partly because I thought I loved him but mostly because marrying him would give me reliable health insurance.

I got pregnant with my daughter in late 2008. When I was 5 months pregnant with her, we went on our honeymoon to Las Vegas. My feet swelled up from all the walking, and I got to watch him get drunk at a different restaurant every night for five days. After that, he told me I was too fat to be attractive to him (there was a baby inside me, you know) and he refused to have sex with me. I had my daughter in 2009, and she tore my vulva to pieces. I ended up in pelvic floor therapy for 6 months, during which time he got out of the Navy and we moved to California. By the time I was physically capable of having sex again, I wanted nothing to do with him. But I was stuck. We moved to Massachusetts so he could get a better job, and my mother would be closer to help us with the kids.

Every time I slept with him, I was drunk. In late 2011, I got pregnant with my son while still married to my first husband. He treated me the same way my father figures had treated me: I was a tool for making babies and taking care of his home life, but I was entitled to no financial benefits because "I didn't work." I was just glad I got to stay home and raise my kids. We decided to have an "open relationship" because we didn't like each other anymore but wanted to stay married for the kids.

Eventually in late 2013, I met the man who would become my second husband. His name was Nate and he was literally half the size of my first husband, but with glasses and a wiry frame covered in muscles. He wanted someone to tell him what to do rather than the other way around. He treated me well and helped me any way he could rather than degrading me and forcing me to get drunk and fuck him (like my ex). I fell hard and fast and decided to divorce my first husband. That was another nightmare.

I knew (because I'd been paying the bills for years) that my ex couldn't afford to keep the house and pay for me to move out at the same time. So I looked for alternatives. I discovered farm apprenticeship, where you live and work on a farm for a whole season. I searched and went on interviews and finally found one that hired me.

I had been a stay-at-home mom for over four years. My kids were my life. I was still going through the paperwork, classes, and mediation of my divorce but I arranged to move to the farm and live there from April through the end of the season. My ex would keep the kids in daycare while he went to work, and I would get to see them one and a half days a month.

The day I arrived at the farm with a carload of my necessities was the hardest day of my life up until that point. I had never been away from my kids more than a day or so. I knew I wouldn't see them for a week. I cried SO. HARD. But I got through it.

I worked my ass off 50-60 hours a week as a farm apprentice. I was 30 years old. I became more fit that season than I had been in my entire life. I got into the rhythm of seeing my kids once a week. When they came to stay with me on the farm (I had my own mini apartment above the garage) I discovered that was the only time they were spending outdoors. My son was inconsolable when I left them with their father, knowing he would be locked inside the house all week. There was nothing I could do.

I got through it. Eventually Nate came to work on the farm with me. He had nothing to his name, and I convinced him to get a bank account and eventually started telling him what to do. He wanted someone to give him orders and I fit the bill. After my apprenticeship ended, I finally finished the divorce process and moved in with the other man.

Every consecutive job I had in the following 8 years was on a farm or in a nursery. That apprenticeship set me up with the skills that I still use to this day. Three years after we moved in with each other the second man and I were married, just after buying a house together in Connecticut. He helped me turn this property into a working farm, however small. He always did what I asked and we never argued. I thought it was the perfect relationship.

Almost every weekend we would do some work on our farm and then get together with friends to drink. Around 2015, I started drinking alcohol every afternoon and more excessively every weekend. I never thought I was an alcoholic. But I realize now that not being able to relax in the afternoon without alcohol fit the bill. And I was drinking more and more to cover up how unhappy I was beneath the surface.

In 2021, my son was 8, my daughter was 12, I was working part time for my stepfather's business and part time at a local small farm as well as building my own farm business up. My husband had gone through HVAC school (upon my insistence) and was working on his Journeyman's license at a full-time position.

I had started visiting my friend Marie on her nearby farm to join in Native American drum circles. I even made my own deer hide drum in the summer of 2021 that I could play at the circles.

My inner self was drowning my unhappiness with whiskey every night and seeking answers to my problems from everyone and everything I could think of. What god would answer my prayers? Could I call in the help of Native elders to answer my questions? How could I become a spirit communicator? Who could teach me how to speak with the dead and get the answers to all my questions? Was I an Indigenous medicine woman in a past life?

This is where my mind was when it all began. I was searching for enlightenment from an indigenous ghost. Where would I find him?

A Secret Graveyard

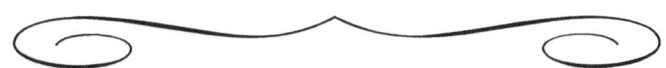

At the time, I worked for a couple in their 60s. Wendy was blonde, a bit shorter than me, and a bit heavyset, her husband Rick was tall and sharp – still chopping wood with an axe regularly.

One day in late April, as I finished my day of hauling mulch for their farm, Wendy came up to me and asked, "By the way, did I ever tell you about the Native American graveyard we have out back in the woods?"

I did a double take. I was expecting her to say goodbye for the day and hand me my pay, not open my curiosity like a garage door. At this point, I had been working for them for two years, so this was certainly news to me.

"What?! No … Where is it?" I asked, immediately interested.

She smiled. "It's down the trail out back, between the turnaround and Grandfather field. I can show you tomorrow afternoon, I'm sure Jason will want to join us." Jason was the young hippie guy who had recently started working with us one day a week as an extra set of hands.

I nodded excitedly. "Deal! I'll plan on staying an hour after work. Thank you!"

She smiled knowingly and let me head home in my truck for the day.

When I got home, I told Nate what Wendy had told me. He was able to pick the kids up from school the following day and he always wanted me to be happy, so we made the schedule change so that I could stay late after work.

The following afternoon I got to work and went about my 4-hour workday as normal. Jason and I hauled branches out of the field and into the burn pile, weeded and cleaned up blackberry beds, and mulched the pathways with fresh wood chips. Typical springtime farm chores.

4 o'clock came and it was time to call it quits. Wendy and Rick joined us for the short walk into the forest to the site. My heart raced in anticipation! The leaves were just barely coming out on the trees, but it was warm that day and I didn't need a coat. I had helped Rick clean up the path before, not knowing where it led, until we veered off onto a different path that I had not known was there.

Little did I realize then that I would soon know those woods as intimately as I knew the backs of my hands. We continued down the wooded trail, deep with brown oak leaves and pine needles, until we saw a large pile of rocks at the V-section of the path. Rick told me that pile marked the other path toward the graveyard. We followed him to the right and up ahead a large hemlock tree loomed. Wendy told us that was where she performed her nature rituals on full moon nights. I smiled, totally understanding how special that spot would be. She had hung streamers from the branches in several places from her last offering.

Just fifty feet or so later, the path opened up into a wide circle. A stack of stones stood before me, neatly in a pile. I could see a similar stack of stones off to the right, then another opposite to the one we were near, and a slightly short stack to the left.

The four corners.

Just past the stack of stones was the pièce de resistance: an offering stone shaped like an arrowhead.

It was a thing of beauty! And it was clearly a natural stone, not shaped by the hands of men. It sat perfectly perched upon some smaller stones, surprisingly sturdy for such an ancient thing.

"We had the Nipmuc tribe out here a few years ago as well as the Archaeological society for the state," Rick said as he leaned on the hoe he had brought so he could push sticks and roots out of our way on the trail. "The Nipmuc couldn't officially say that this was from their tribe, but they didn't seem to know very much. They said it looked like a site for ceremonies because of the offering stone and the tall stacks which match North, South, East, and West almost perfectly. And the state archaeologist told us that it would be more trouble than it was worth to have the spot fully investigated. So, we went to the town hall and created a land trust so this portion of our property could never be developed."

I stood there in awe, nodding at the story. It was a reverent place.

Rick, Wendy, Jason, and I poked around the site a little longer before Rick asked us if we wanted to see the natural spring down the trail a little way.

"Of course!" I said. We followed him down a different winding trail until we got to a small open pool where we could hear gently running water. Stones had been stacked in an oval shape creating a natural watering hole for animals and the ideal spot for a big patch of wild watercress to grow.

The water bubbled up from the ground, filling the pool from deep within the earth, then the excess ran down a tiny stream further down the trail toward an area that was farmland centuries before.

I leaned down and grabbed a small piece of watercress and put it into my mouth. It was peppery and tasted fresh, one of the nicest things I had ever eaten.

Rick said that Native people on the land had used it as a water source for centuries before colonizers took their land, at which point the spring had been repurposed into a watering hole for cows. It had been laying untouched in this state since the late 1800s when the property was sold and allowed to grow wooded again.

Rick told me he thought I would get sick because I hadn't washed it first but I said "This stream is fed up from the earth and we're deep in the woods where virtually no one has been for over a hundred years. I don't think it's polluted."

I was fine. Not even a tummy grumble.

After ooh-ing and ahh-ing over the natural water source, they led us back through the forest to Grandfather field, where I had a small garden space that I rented on their land. I checked on my garlic that was coming up from having been planted in fall and then we all walked back up the main trail toward the house.

That day was the beginning of the biggest revolution of my life thus far.

3

Building Up a Dream

My version of a "normal" life was working my two jobs throughout the week, tending my small farm's gardens and poultry, learning more about herbs and foraging, and spending as much time as I could in nature.

I had an affinity for identifying plants and I was building relationships with the ones I saw every day. I treated the natural world as my church and Mother Earth as my deity. Yet still I did not feel whole. I could see my house and my family, but I couldn't see my future with them. I kept searching for answers and I thought that perhaps the Native People in their wisdom would have some for me.

I was vending at one farmer's market every month with my handmade herbal incense, canned foods such as jellies and salsa that I made on my farm, and whatever vegetables I had growing in excess that week.

I was also spending any free weekends I had with my

friend Marie anywhere we could find a drum circle. In late May, she had a huge yard sale at her house and invited me and a few other friends to set up our vendor booths in her large yard so we could sell our own yard sale items and some of our handmade wares as well.

I was having a great time selling my handmade stuff and making a little extra cash by selling some other things I had brought from home. During a lull in the traffic, I showed her the photos of the Native Ceremonial site.

"Holy cow, I need to see this!" she exclaimed, very excited. Her tiny frame bounced and her eyes lit up. "You know Ann from the Town Hall? I just found out that her husband is half Native American and an actual shaman!"

My jaw dropped. "No way! I've known Ann for years, she never told me that."

Marie nodded emphatically. "We're going to have to get you in touch with him, he's going to want to see that place. And my boyfriend Ray knows another shaman we can ask about it too. He does soul readings."

I had no idea what that meant, but someone had gone over to my booth to check out my jellies, and I rushed back to take care of them.

The yard sale event eventually ended and the following day I texted Marie about meeting up with Ann and her shaman husband. Since I knew Ann, she was happy to introduce me.

The following week, we got together at Marie's house for a drum circle. Ann showed up just after I had arrived and out of her SUV stepped a huge, looming old man.

Dan was easily six-foot-four and a heavyset man in his late 60s. He had trouble with one of his legs and needed support by leaning on a tall wooden staff he carried with him for the purpose. He wore glasses and had neatly trimmed gray hair and a very kind face.

He gave me a hug when he met me for the first time. I took an instant liking to him.

Ann stood beside him, an older white woman about the same height as me with short, bright red dyed hair, a sharp but cheerful expression perpetually on her face.

The four of us talked about Dan's native background. He had worked as a surveyor for several towns due to his uncanny ability to douse water pipes and waterways unseen below the ground. He told us about some of his travels all over New England, having met and spoken with many tribes and discovered many ancient medicine man burial sites. Some sites had cursed the white men who had bulldozed them over in the name of progress, causing them to sicken rapidly with sudden strange illnesses and in some cases, cancer.

His stories fascinated me and he was full of them! He became a friend whom I sought out time and again for advice.

I told Dan and Ann about the native ceremonial site at the farm I worked on and they were intrigued. So, I asked Wendy and Rick if they would mind me bringing visitors down to the site. They trusted my judgment and gave me the go ahead, so we scheduled a time for all of us to go exploring.

A few days ahead of our excursion, Rick and I went down to the site with weed whackers and cleaned up the excessive amounts of lady ferns covering the ground. He whacked the greenery down while I cleared the area of debris like large branches that had fallen and covered some of the stone piles. The whole ceremonial area was about 100 feet wide, so it wasn't an enormous undertaking but still took us about an hour to accomplish.

This was when I learned an interesting fact: Native people built stone walls. The stone wall that ran around the ceremonial site snaked and wound and looked very old. Rick told me it was older than the taller, newer colonial stone walls that were further down the field.

In our clearing work, I accidentally tripped over a stone. Then another one close by. When Rick cleared the ferns, I realized what we had found. "Oh my god, look over here!" I shouted, waving him over in my direction. He looked down at the ground as I pointed.

"Here... then here... and here..." I walked around in a complete circle, pointing out all the stones that marked it. "I think I just found a medicine wheel!"

Rick's eyebrows went up. "Neat," he said carefully. "What does that mean?" Rick didn't know a lot about Indigenous religious practices, but I had been studying them for some time and was happy to explain.

"It's a ceremonial circle they used to mark the seasons and celebrate the equinoxes," I explained. "There are thirteen stones in a circle here, at least I think there are." I poked the ground with my toe. "This one is kind of buried so I'm not 100% sure. But these are clearly set in a circle. Can't you see it?"

He nodded. I could see that Rick wasn't super interested but he helped me clear the site better so that everyone would be able to see it when I brought them down. Once we were satisfied that the site was all visible, we headed back up and ended our workday.

The day came and I brought Nate with me, as he came from a part Native background (Menomonee in Wisconsin). Dan and Ann arrived, and Marie was right on their heels. I introduced them to my boss, and we chatted for a few minutes about how the summer heat was really coming early this June before we set off toward the historic site.

I led everyone down the path (Wendy and Rick were too busy to join us) and we walked carefully so that Dan wouldn't trip on anything along the way. He leaned on his staff, and I kept turning back to check on him, even

Uncovering *Amy*

though Nate was walking behind him to help make certain he didn't fall.

The dappled sunlight filtered through the tree canopy gently. It was warm for June but not sweltering yet. The matted path of pine needles and humus was pleasant beneath our feet and every now and then a light breeze would waft over us.

Dan was already dripping sweat from his forehead. I was pretty sure he wasn't used to being out in the heat anymore since he had retired a few years ago. Ann kept up with me, chatting pleasantly about one of the native Archaeological sites she had visited up in New Hampshire previously.

As we made our way past the sacred hemlock tree, my heart beat a little faster in anticipation of Dan seeing the site. Then the ferns opened up and the south facing stone was before us.

I was glad that Rick had helped me clear the ferns from the site itself because the place was opulent in its full summer greenery, even with shorter ferns. Everyone took a moment to admire the scene before we went over to the offering stone.

Ann reached into her small hip pouch that she was wearing and pulled out two plastic tubes and two metal rods that were bent into an "L" shape. She set the metal rods inside the plastic tubing and held one in each hand.

"What are those?" I asked, reaching out to touch one gently.

She smiled knowingly. "They're dowsing rods. Dan is an expert at them and I'm pretty good too."

Dan came over and grinned down at me. "These are the easy kind," he said in his loud but gentle timbre. "If I'm in a pinch, I can just break off a witch hazel branch that's about that same shape and use it just as easily. Not every-body can do that, though."

"What do you need to dowse for?" I asked. "I can show you the natural spring after we're finished but there's no water right here." I gestured toward the other stones.

Now Dan's smile turned very sly. "I can use these for SO much more than just finding water." He took the rods that Ann offered him after setting his walking stick up against a nearby ash tree.

My brows furrowed quizzically and his smile expanded even more. He held the rods out before him, his arms held evenly apart. "I can use these to communicate with the spirits of the dead."

My eyeballs must have looked like I just stuck my finger in a light socket because Dan laughed, wiping the sweat from his brow with his left arm. The fat on his neck jig-gled when he laughed and made him appear all the more jolly.

"How do they work?" I asked, intrigued. I was standing

Uncovering *Amy*

before him near a tree while Ann wandered toward one of the other stone piles.

He held the two rods out in front of him, his elbows curled. The plastic tubing was in each hand, but the wire was set loosely inside facing away from him. "You can start by asking yes or no questions," he said. "Like this: is my name Dan?" The wires swung inward, crossing each other. "That's yes. Is Amelia behind me?" The wires swung back outward; the right one swinging to his right and the left one swinging to his left. "Good." He used one hand to gently reset the wires, so they pointed directly in front of him once more. "You can also count numbers by how many times they swing, and they'll point at whatever you're looking for. So, if I'm out looking for a water way under the earth, the wires will point me in the direction to find the nearest underground vein of water."

"Is that what you used to do for the city?" I asked.

He grinned. "Actually, I could find all sorts of underground pipes for them. I remember one time they didn't know where this one antique sewer pipe led to. They gave up on their maps because none of them were accurate for where the manhole covers came out or the drainage let out. They called me in and I traced the pipes about four acres past where they thought they were supposed to be. I told them where to dig, and they located the missing outlet just four feet down.

"Holy crap, they're that accurate?"

Dan's smile turned sly as his gaze went from the divining rods back to me. "More like I'm that accurate."

We began investigating the stone piles one by one. The first one that we had come to, just north of the offering stone, was a direction indicator. It was in the best shape of the four, South, East, and West having been partially deteriorated or knocked over by time and probably random tree branches falling over the years. The next stone pile we came to was more sacred, however.

Dan stood with his arms evenly spaced, holding the rods slightly away from his torso. "He asked a question quietly under his breath.

"What was that?" I asked? Ann was standing not far behind him, and Nate was settled behind her, watching quietly.

"I was deciphering whether or not this pile is a grave," he explained, his face turned down as he concentrated on the pile of stones. He looked up at me over his glasses, a sparkle in his eyes. "It is. And do you see that white quartz stone just there?"

I looked where he gestured and sure enough there was a white quartz stone, about the size of two of my fists, nestled near the top of this meter-high stone pile. "Yeah," I said.

"That means this is the grave of a medicine man."

"Wowwwww," I said in awe, taking a glance back at

Nate. He smiled a bit, seeming impressed.

Dan asked another question. "How old is this grave?" I watched his arms remain stiff in front of him while he asked. The wire in his right hand swung outward and then back in again, like a fan, over and over and over. "One hundred, two hundred, three hundred," Dan counted until it stopped swinging. "Tens?" he asked. The wire swung outward in the "yes" formation. Dan counted until he got to 60. The whole process only took a minute but was fascinating to watch. When he finished, he looked up at me. "This particular grave is over 760 years old."

My jaw dropped. How could this site be so ancient and not be on a protected list somehow?

Dan asked what tribe this site was from next. He started naming tribes from the region until the wires crossed in the "yes" answer again. Ann had wandered back over to where we were at that point, and she looked at him with a smile on her face.

"Nipmuc?" she asked. Dan nodded.

"Makes sense. This was their ancestral land for as long as anyone kept records," she said. She wiped some sweat from the back of her neck and, gesturing behind her, added "There are more graves over this way."

I stopped Dan before he followed her. "How do you know it's a grave?"

He smiled again, one eyebrow rising over the rim of his silver glasses. "It's actually really interesting," he explained, picking up his walking stick again and readjusting his weight to lean on it.

"When someone of importance died, notably a medicine man or woman, the tribe would leave their body in the forest, exposed to the elements. Animals would come and eat the flesh, then insects would devour what was left. It spread the bones out a bit, but they could still be collected once the human remains were given back to the earth. Someone would come back a few months later and collect the bones, and they would be wrapped in an animal skin very reverently along with some of the medicine person's personal or magical effects. Then a very shallow grave would be dug and the bone package carefully set into it and covered with stones. The people would hold a funeral of sorts where everyone who knew this medicine person or anyone they had ever helped during their life would come to see the grave and leave a stone on top of it. Some graves are still to this day piled very high due to how many people loved and revered that particular medicine man."

I nodded again. "And the Quartz?"

"White quartz is the stone emblem for a medicine person here in New England. We have pockets of it in several places. They would find the biggest chunk of it they could and add that near the top of the stone pile to mark it as the grave of a Medicine person. It is very bad luck to take that stone. Some who have done so have been cursed."

"Kind of like robbing an Egyptian tomb," I said, visibly impressed. Dan nodded.

"Men have gotten sick suddenly with strange illnesses and even cancer shortly after removing quartz from a medicine man's grave or bulldozing the sites over, as I saw in a case up in New Hampshire. Several men who had been responsible for that demolition died and the others were gravely ill before they figured out what was wrong. I was called to consult up there and when I told the man dying of cancer that he had to return the Quartz he rushed to get it done, sick as he was."

"Did he die anyway?" I asked.

"No, actually. His cancer went into remission a month later and he's still alive to this day."

"Holy shit," I said.

Ann gestured from behind me and beckoned us over. Dan and I walked over to her, about thirty feet from the tall grave we had been standing at. "She's old but very important," Ann said, pointing to a stone pile that was spread out wider than the one we had just been looking at. "Definitely a medicine woman and the rods say her grave is over six hundred years old."

Dan held his rods out and asked the grave a few more

questions. He and Ann stood chatting while Nate sat on one of the stones near the medicine wheel.

I walked over toward the edge of the site beside one of the paths to get in from the opposite direction and squatted down beside another stone pile. I reached out my right hand to touch one of the stones on top of the pile gently. Suddenly, I got a sharp, stabbing pain in the back on my head. I lifted my hand quickly and placed it on my head where I felt the pain, but it was gone just as suddenly as it had appeared.

Puzzled, I reached my hand out and touched the stone again. The pain shot back again, slightly weaker, but still just at the back of my skull. I stood up and beckoned Ann over.

"I think this is another grave," I said hesitantly. "Can you check?"

She held her rods out and asked the questions softly. I watched the rods swing yes and no.

"I think he was killed by an arrow or something to the back of his head," I said. "Can you ask him?"

She asked. The rods swung vehemently yes!

Ann's eyebrows rose. "I felt his pain when I touched the stones," I explained.

"That's definitely a sign that you're meant to communicate and connect with them," she said approvingly.

Next, I showed them the medicine wheel, and we walked all over the site, reading grave piles for their age. Dan even doused an answer to the site itself—it was over 1000 years old and had been used as a ceremonial place for hundreds of years. They stopped using it sometime around the late 1600s when Colonial farmers took over the land and drove them out. Dan said there were at least 50 graves all over the property here, most of them medicine men.

"The interesting thing to me is that it's lasted all these years, even after the Natives left," I said, still awestruck.

"Well, you have to remember that the Colonists were pretty superstitious. Even they knew that a spot like this held sacred meaning," Dan explained. "They probably built their farms all around this, but they would have known better than to take the stone graves down. And if a farmer's family owned this area for a couple generations, that's all it would take to get overgrown and just become another part of the woods."

I stood there, staring at the site around me. Nate was mostly quiet during our visit. He was there more because of me than due to any interest he had. His own tribe was in the Midwest, far from here.

"Let's go see the spring before we head back," I suggested. Dan was getting tired, but Ann handed him her water bottle, and he steadied himself on his walking stick once again.

I led us all single file away from the site and down the path where Rick had shown me the fresh bubbling spring. I leaned down to check the watercress, but it had all gone to seed and wasn't good to eat anymore.

"You can see where the stones used to be over here," Dan said, pointing his stick behind the circular opening. "This was probably where the local tribe got their water until the Colonials arrived. Then some farmer turned it into a cow watering hole."

"It's a shame to be going to waste like this, considering it's such fresh beautiful water." Ann and Dan looked at each other after I said this, giving a look of "I wouldn't trust it," to each other silently. I shrugged. I was a forager and ate wild things all the time, so it was no stretch for me to consider drinking from a wild spring, but they were used to city water and plumbing.

"We'd better head back, I don't think Dan can hold out for much longer," Ann suggested. We all turned back and headed up the trail toward the house once more.

"You see why I was so excited now?" I asked. They all agreed that it was a wonderful place and they would like to return sometime.

We made it back to the driveway and chatted for a while with Wendy and Rick about the site. They were quite impressed with what Dan told them about its history.

"Well we're going to keep it preserved as long as we live here and it's in the land trust so no one can harm it," Wendy assured him.

Ann and Dan both smiled. "This place is a treasure," Ann said to them, before she looked at me. "I'm sure Amelia can help you take care of it."

"She is," Rick assured them.

And with that, we all loaded into our respective vehicles and went home for the day.

Spiritual Influencers

The remainder of summer went by in a flash for me. Working on someone else's farm as well as my own along with homesteading and making products to bring to markets is an incredibly busy lifestyle.

I visited the Sanctuary once or twice, and I kept feeling the pull, but July and August were simply packed with activity as it was harvesting and canning season. I was also making new friends as I delved deeper into shamanic healing and attended drum circles regularly. I even made my own deer hide drum!

I also visited with Dan several times. His health was going downhill, but he was always eager to converse about Native history and communication, and he loved telling me stories of the adventures he used to have as a land surveyor.

On one of our visits, he loaned me a book called Mutant Message Down Under[1], a story about a white woman who traveled to Australia and was taken on walkabout by an Aboriginal Tribe which showed her how to live in harmony with the earth and how to communicate telepathically with other humans. It was an interesting read and opened my eyes to the possibility that I could potentially learn to communicate telepathically one day (this idea will be important later).

He also showed me his impressive shoe box full of arrow heads and other indigenous artifacts that he had found and collected over the years. He even let me take one!

He had many arrowheads in varying shapes, colors, and types of stone but I was drawn to the quartz. I especially like to think that the teeny line of rusty orange may be ingrained from the arrowhead being used to kill an animal, but that could just be a fanciful idea on my part.

The more I learned from Dan the deeper into American Indian folklore and beliefs I sank. I found myself hoping that someday I could connect with my Native ancestors. I knew that my great-grandmother belonged to the Osage tribe and that my cousin had contacted them once to verify our shared ancestry, but I had personally never had any opportunity to connect with that minute side of my heritage.

I was honestly wishing I was one of them instead of the white woman I actually am.

One day in August I wanted to try connecting with some kind of nature spirits, hoping I would receive answers from the spirit world about my personal destiny. I took a walk in one of the nearby state parks, down a back path I hadn't traveled often before.

The day was hot, birdsong and a few random cicada sounds in the air, but the shade over the path felt cool and I knew it followed the stream. No sooner had I descended a small hill into the deeper part of the woods than I chose to look up at just the right time. I looked over the stream toward a small island in the middle of it and saw a beautiful snowy owl staring down at me from a tree branch.

My jaw opened like a fish gasping for air as we stared at each other for a solid minute. My mind was racing—what does this mean? Every animal or major natural event has symbolic meaning in Native cultures, so I reached into my pocket for my smart phone and quickly Googled "spiritual meaning of seeing a white owl."

Just as the answers began to populate in my search, I looked up in time to watch the owl jump off the branch and fly toward me, veering off to my left as I watched it in awe.

I looked down again after I lost sight of him and my search query had been answered:

Seeing a white owl is often interpreted as a positive omen, symbolizing spiritual awakening, wisdom, and purity.

Uncovering *Amy*

Spiritual Meaning of a White Owl

The white owl is known for sending spiritual signs and symbols that are meant to help you connect with yourself spiritually and to help you work past the struggles in your life so you can connect with the present moment.

They are spiritual creatures that mark the beginning and end of things so you can pay attention to things that you've learned so far and then grow from them.[2]

"Holy hell," I said quietly under my breath, my heart racing as I listened to the quiet babbling of the stream.

I knew this was going to be an important day. I walked a little further down the trail, glad that it was the middle of the day on my day off and I didn't have to worry about picking my kids up from somewhere. I removed my flip flops and held them in one hand; glad I was wearing shorts as I eyed the bank of the little island looking for a good spot to enter.

I stepped carefully into the stream, letting out a little sigh as the cool water touched my warm legs. I had to place each step carefully, watching through the slowly running water to decide where to set my foot down among the slippery rocks at the bottom. The water was only up to just below my knees, but a wrong step could cause me and my small bag of stuff to crash right into the water. I made it across the thirty-foot span safely, reaching out for a long root that extended from the bank where the soil from the island had washed away, and I climbed up.

I looked around for a minute or two. The island was only about twelve feet wide but probably 80 feet long. I was covered in the same trees, moss, and ground covers as the rest of the forest, just in its own little world surrounded by the stream on both sides. I picked a spot near the bank to sit so that the running water would help clear my head and I settled in to meditate.

I'll be honest with you now: I've never thought I was good at meditating. I have a hard time releasing thoughts from my head and making everything go quiet. But I did my best to focus on the sounds of nature all around me. I even laid down for a little while, urging myself to take a nap. Eventually, a new song popped into my head and I sat upright quickly. I sang it into the recording app on my phone and then sat for a while longer, pleased that "something" had come through.

Eventually, after about an hour and a half of attempting to communicate with Spirit, I packed myself up and crossed the stream again to walk back to my truck. I wasn't really certain what had happened, but the owl told me it was important.

I went home, made dinner, and finished the evening as normal.

About two weeks later, I received a call from Marie. "Ray told me about this Native American shaman he knows in Ashford," she said with excitement in her voice. "He offered to do shamanic spirit readings for all of us over at Ray's house this weekend. Dan and Ann are joining us to get readings too. Are you in?"

I thought about it for a minute, wondering if I could afford the inevitable fee, and said "Hell yes! I'll do it! Just give me the time and address."

She did so and told me that the guy was only charging us $30 each to do the readings so I was grateful I could afford it.

The day came and I drove over to Ray's house. Ray was an older man with Cherokee heritage that Marie had been dating for several months. His house was clean and neat with several interesting Native American-inspired art pieces on his walls. After I walked inside, I was introduced to the shaman, a corpulent Native American man of virtually indistinguishable age with graying dark long hair and a pockmarked face. He wore a black t-shirt and jeans and had several necklaces on including a medicine bag with some porcupine quills attached to the leather sack and one with what looked like alligator teeth on it, causing it to look like a weird collar for his shirt.

"This is my friend Randy," Ray said by way of introduction. Ray was a tall, decent-looking guy in his 60s who let off an air of know-it-all-ness that I wasn't particularly fond of, but I wasn't here to argue with anyone. I smiled and shook Randy's outstretched hand, not knowing what to think.

"Hi, I'm Amelia," I said awkwardly. He gave me a strained smile. I could tell he wasn't much of a people person.

"We're all going to wait outside on the back deck while everyone takes turns talking with Randy alone so they can have privacy for their reading," Ray said. "He's all set up in the living room over here."

"I'll go first!" Marie said excitedly.

Randy nodded. I handed him my $30 in cash then, so I wouldn't forget, as did the others. Then I went out to the deck with everyone else and sat in one of Ray's lawn chairs to wait for my own turn.

Dan regaled Ann, Ray, and me with more tales of his exploits working with various native tribes while we waited. The majority of the deck was in the shade and afternoon had set in nicely, so it felt like a relaxing day with old friends. I even hopped up to check out Ray's herb garden, which had a substantial plot of Sweetgrass growing in one of the raised beds.

Eventually, Marie came out to the deck to join us. "What was it like?" I asked her eagerly, my eyes lit up with excitement.

She seemed both unnerved and slightly disappointed.

"It was enlightening for sure," she said, trying to sound excited. I could tell something was off, but I didn't say anything in front of Dan and Ann. "Do you want to go next?"

"Absolutely!" I couldn't contain my excitement. Even if she didn't like what she heard from Randy, that didn't mean I was going to have the same experience. I jumped out of my chair, which Marie then took over, and went inside the house.

Randy was waiting for me inside. When he saw me coming, he smiled and gestured to the next room. I followed him there and sat down in a big overstuffed blue armchair while he settled himself in another chair beside me.

"You can record our session with an app on your phone if you like," he suggested gently. "That way you can listen to it again later in case you forget anything."

"Good idea," I said, pulling out my phone to search for a suitable recording app. I found one after a minute or so and tested it, then asked if he was ready. He nodded and I hit record, setting the phone on the arm rest while I turned my attention to him.

He closed his eyes and looked toward the ceiling. "Thank you, Ancestors, for allowing me to be a conduit through which your messages may flow. Great spirits, I ask you to give your message for Amelia through me." Then he said something in his native language that I didn't understand and he turned his head, his eyes slightly glazed over as if he was looking through me rather than at me.

> *[I'll be honest with you, reader: I no longer have the recording of this session and while it lasted about 30 minutes, I don't remember everything he told me. I'm giving you the highlights that I remember here.]*

"You are Nipmuc," he began. "You have Nipmuc in you."

"Really?" I asked, astonished. "I knew my great-grandmother was Osage, but I've never heard of any Nipmuc tribal members in my bloodline."

He looked to his right and swallowed. I thought maybe he seemed a little nervous, but I wanted to hear more.

"You are wolf medicine. You're here to be a powerful healer. I see blue and white light around you. There's a big flat rock in your backyard that you must meditate on to connect with Spirit."

I thought for a minute. There's a patch of wooded area, about a quarter of an acre, at the rear part of my property. Nate and I had set up a haunted trail there for Halloween during the Covid lockdown so I knew the big flat rock that was back there, partly covered in brambles, where I had set up a fake skeleton on the ground with another fake skeleton stabbing him with a big fake knife as part of the display.

This guy whom I had never met before today knew about that big rock in my back woods? How?! And he said I was a healer … I had just begun seeing clients as an herbalist this year! This was some heavy shit. My heart was racing with excitement.

"You are to look for a sign from Spirit. It will be a big bird."

"I have been seeing a heron frequently on my drive to work. And I just saw a huge white owl last week right before I meditated in the forest. Are they giving me a message?" I asked, hopeful the answer was yes.

He nodded. "Yes, Spirit connects to you in any way they can. You're meant to do great things in this life."

[The reading went on, with me eagerly fitting whatever he said into the puzzle pieces of my mind. While some things he told me seemed specific, I realize now while writing this that the guy was able to tell me exactly what I wanted to hear by giving me broad generalizations enough that I, in my naiveté, would fit it all together into my life and believe whatever he fed me like a fish living in a barrel. It's clear now that he was a shyster. I look back on this experience with the wisdom I have now and shudder. I am so grateful that someone like this would not be able to take advantage of my hopes and beliefs anymore!]

Finally, he took a deep sigh and said "That is all Spirit has to tell you today. We are glad to help." Then he closed his eyes again, said something else in his Native tongue that sounded like a prayer, and opened his eyes. He gave me what seemed like a forced, strained smile, and told me that my next step should be to make a medicine wheel with porcupine quills. He even had some in his bag that he gave me, extras from a craft project he had started. He told me where I could find instructions on how to construct it online and sent me off with it, waiting for the next person in line for their reading.

I left the room and went out to the deck again to sit down with Marie and Dan, sending Ann in for her reading.

I was buzzing with the thrill of my reading. I just knew it meant that I was on the right path to being a medicine woman, just like the ones buried at the Sanctuary in the woods! I talked with Marie and Dan about what the shaman had told me.

We continued chatting until everyone had had their reading and then we said our goodbyes and went home.

With all this encouragement, native spirits dancing in my head, and Dan's stories of working with indigenous people swimming around at will, it's no wonder what happened next was both astonishing and expected all at once.

 Uncovering *Amy*

I didn't know it yet, but my life was about to get really weird.

THE AWAKENING

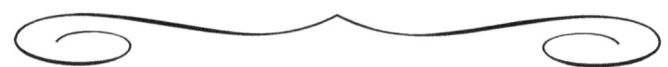

Near the end of August, I began visiting the site as often as I could spare. On one occasion, I brought a notebook and my phone and sat inside the medicine wheel to meditate.

I was desperate to be able to communicate with the spirits of the medicine men and women there. I felt like I was meant to be there, to find that place, and to protect it with my life. I felt like I was one of them.

I sat on the ground with my back up against a rock facing east for around 40 minutes, my eyes closed, listening to the birds and the wind gently blowing through the trees. The midday sun sparkled through the tree canopy and a light breeze made the warm forest air more comfortable than oppressive.

I opened my eyes and looked up. Across the ceremony circle, just beyond the big hemlock tree, a coyote walked up. We stared at each other for nearly two solid minutes, him trying to decide whether I was a threat and me internally freaking out as to whether I should stay where I was or get up and run.

Finally, he looked straight ahead of him down the path that led back into the woods and decided it wasn't worth going past me. He turned around and trotted back the way he came silently, and I breathed a sigh of relief.

Then I went to my smart phone to Google the meaning:

"Another thing to consider is that a coyote is often depicted as a trickster in lore and legend. This is not always a bad thing, but you might want to show some caution in your day-to-day life and decisions."[3]

If that wasn't ominous and foreboding, I'm not sure what would be.

As September began, Nate and I had a weekend out with friends and took the kids on a long hike. The days were still sunny and warm, and I was feeling more comfortable than ever in the forest since I'd been spending so much time there.

That Monday I went to work at the farm as usual. After my shift was over, I walked down to the Sanctuary to meditate for a while. This time, I brought out the set of dowsing rods that Dan had made for me. I took off my flip flops, sat beside the large grave of the 600-year-old medicine man and began asking him some questions.

I held the rods out at arm's length and said out loud, "Do you like it when I come to visit with you?"

The wires crossed. Yes!

I asked a few other questions, getting yes or no answers. I was having such a good time actually conversing with a spirit that I was running out of ways I could ask yes or no questions. I found myself wishing that I could ask and receive a different kind of answer somehow.

The sky had begun to turn gray, and I had felt a few sprinkles on the back of my neck, but I wasn't worried. The forecast on my phone said it might rain a bit, but I wasn't too far of a walk from my truck so I could put a stop to my visit at any time.

I thought of a new question to ask. "Do you know the other medicine men here?"

Yes.

"Do you know where the other graves are?"

Yes.

"Can you tell me?"

Yes.

"How?"

Silence. Then, the wires began spinning around in circles. My brow furrowed. "What the hell does that mean?" I asked myself.

I thought for a minute. "Can you show me from where I'm sitting?"

No.

"Do you want me to stand up?"

YES!!! [The wires spun so quickly toward yes]

I could tell the spirit was excited.

Unsure of how this was going to play out, I stood up. I was barefoot in the woods still, but I held the wires out.

NO.

No wires? How would I know what he was saying? "Should I close my eyes?" YES. YES.

I held the wires at my side and stood there with my eyes closed. Nothing happened. What the hell are you doing, Amelia? This is ridiculous.

Then I felt it.

A slight push, as if someone had their hand on my back and was nudging me forward. I took a breath and let my shoulders sink. I released the tension in my body and let myself sway a bit, as if I was a twig dangling off a tree controlled by nothing but the wind.

Push.

There it was again!

PUSH.

I lurched forward, opening my eyes just in time to catch myself from falling on my face.

"Wait just a minute!" I exclaimed, standing up straight again. I relaxed my tension and felt outward with my senses.

Then it happened. It felt as if there were hands on each of my shoulders, gently pushing me forward. I let go of control and allowed my feet to go where they wanted to, following the push. At first, it pushed me into a big pile of branches. Then it slammed me into a big stone in the ground.

"Listen," I said gently but firmly. "I'm okay with you guiding me somewhere but please remember that I have feet and I need to walk around big things like that."

I held the wires up for a moment and they quickly crossed yes, as if in apology. I could sense the excitement from the being; he was as eager to show me where he wanted me to go as I was to experience it.

A light drizzle began to fall but I didn't care. This was beyond thrilling and I wasn't going to stop just because of a little rain! I had left my shoes back inside the ceremony circle, but my feet were tough enough from farming to withstand the leaves and sticks on the forest floor. Being barefoot in the forest, pushed around by a dead Native American medicine man was beyond anything I could have put on my personal bucket list and I was here for it.

The force pushed me a good 30 feet into the woods, away from any path, behind where the original grave was. It stopped me right in front of another stone pile. This one was wider and flatter, not stacked up like "his" grave was. It could have just been a big pile of rocks that had been sitting there for a few hundred years.

I held the rods out and asked, "Is this a grave?"

Yes.

"It this one older than yours?"

Yes.

"How much older?"

The rods began to swing back and forth, just as I had seen Dan's rods do when he was visiting the site with me. One, two, three four, five, six, seven, then slooooowly stop.

"Over 700 years old?"

Yes.

I pulled a small piece of white quartz stone from my

pocket. I had collected a handful of them at the beach in July and brought them with me to set on the three medicine person graves as a gift to the spirits. I had done that before I sat down to chat with the 600-year-old spirit, but I had a few left still.

I set the quartz gently on top of the rock pile and said "I see you and I honor you. You are not forgotten."

I stood up and felt the push from behind again. "Okay, I'm going, I'm going! Jeez Louise," I said. It pushed me in another direction, closer to the trail this time. It stopped me at another pile of stones, this one slightly taller but distinct.

I repeated the same questioning as before. "Is this a grave?"

Yes.

"I see you and I honor you. You are not forgotten." And I placed another quartz stone down.

The pushing became more insistent, as did the rain. The force shoved me along, wandering this way and that through the woods in all directions. I ran out of quartz stones from my pocket by the time I got to the 7th grave.

"I'm sorry, I'm out of stone offerings. I can go to the beach again and get more. Are there more graves you want to show me?"

YES!

So, I went with it. The force pushed me, zig-zagging around the woods, and stopping at every pile of rocks both big and small, for at least thirty minutes in the drizzling rain.

By the time it pushed me toward the circle, he had shown me over 60 grave piles. I was flabbergasted! I reminded him that I was sorry to not have brought more stones, but I certainly had not been expecting to be introduced to so many deceased medicine men.

"I need to go home now, is that okay?"

Yes.

"I'll come back and see you again soon, I promise!"

Yes.

My heart was racing with the thrill of what had just happened. I gathered my things and trudged up the trail back toward my truck, flip flops in hand. When I arrived at the driveway, Wendy was there.

"You're not gonna BELIEVE what just happened!" I exclaimed, my hands vibrating with excitement. She looked at me quizzically.

I told her about the force talking to me and pushing me around the forest, showing me all the graves of various medicine men. Her eyebrows were up, very surprised.

"That's really very cool," she said in the end, mildly impressed. This wasn't her thing, I guess. I was excited and that's all that counted.

"I'll be back again tomorrow," I said. "I'll be back as often as I can. I love it here!" She smiled back at me as I got into my truck and left for home.

Nate was never going to believe this. I don't know who would. But the rods didn't lie. I was speaking with the dead.

A Month of
Communication and Love

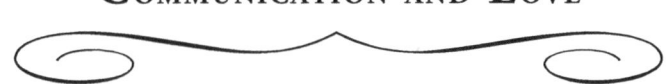

For the next week, I spent as many hours at the Sanctuary as I could. I would go to work at the farm and as soon as my work was finished, I'd walk down the trail into the forest to see my friends, the dead medicine men from hundreds of years past.

Sometimes when I sat with them, I would feel images enter my head, like pictures from a dream. I knew this was their way of communicating with me across time and I was proud of the fact that I had mastered being able to achieve this level of communication with a deceased spirit.

I learned, through sitting and meditating with it, that the one whose grave had shown me that he died from something hitting him in the back of the head had been a mighty warrior as well as a medicine man, wearing the skin of a skunk on his head to protect him during war parties. I called him Skunk Man.

The one who had stood me up and shown me all the nearby graves was a great chief and medicine man of his time. Then there was the elderly medicine woman, whose gravestones were piled about 20 feet to the rear of the chief's.

With the dowsing rods I was able to decipher whether each medicine person was a man or a woman, about how long ago they had died, and I could ask them whether the vision I was seeing (if I had one while I sat by their grave) was from them.

I felt like I was getting to know them in a distant sort of way.

One day as I was sitting on the forest floor with Skunk Man's grave, I got the notion in my head to offer him a snack. I pulled out some dried apricots from my bag and set one on his grave.

"Would you like one?" I asked, then I held the dowsing rods out and waited.

Yes.

I thought for a minute. "But you can't actually eat it, I know."

Yes.

I thought again. A crazy idea came into my head, but I figured it just might work.

"I don't know if this is possible, but could you maybe come inside my body for a minute and then you can use my mouth to taste the apricot? I bet you miss food."

YES. YES. YES.

I chuckled. "Okay, I give you permission to come into my body for long enough to eat a snack."

Silence. I waited. I didn't really feel any different, so I asked out loud. "Want to eat?"

Yes! I heard the voice inside my own head this time. Whoa, that was wild! I picked a dried apricot out of my bag and ate it slowly, savoring the flavor.

"Was that good?" I asked out loud again after I swallowed. I grabbed another and put it into my mouth.

I ate four apricots with the spirit inside me before I finally said, "That's enough now. My body doesn't need any more. Go back now."

I don't want to.

"Come on now, this was the agreement. Please be kind to me."

Okay.

Another minute passed and I didn't really feel any different, but I asked, "Are you back in your grave now?"

I felt and heard nothing, so I picked up the rods.

Yes.

I smiled. "Good. I'm glad I was able to give you that treat. I have to get going now.

Yes.

I'll say goodbye to everyone, and I'll be back in a few days."

Yes.

I stood up from the ground and made my rounds to say goodbye to the other graves. Then I gathered my things and went home.

Two days later I was driving home, windows open on a warm September evening, from another drum circle at my friend's house. I was riding the spiritual high of the drums, feeling connected to everything around me even though I was still in my truck. As I turned onto the road that brought me nearly home, I suddenly smelled a dead skunk in the wind.

At first, I thought nothing of it. I'm sure you smelled that distinctive skunk odor on a road near you after someone accidentally hit a skunk. But after a few seconds, my heart dropped. My eyes opened wide.

It was a sign.

Uncovering *Amy*

"Oh my god," I said out loud, trying to concentrate most of my attention on the road. "Are you still inside my head?"

I felt an inward sensation of something like guilty glee. Yes.

My heart leaped into my throat. "You've been inside my head this whole time?"

Haha, yes. Sorry I did not tell you.

I sighed. "Are you going to leave?"

No.

"Freaking great."

I drove the rest of the way home thinking silently. What was I supposed to do? Had I been possessed? It didn't feel evil. It didn't feel wrong. It just felt like I was talking to my friend, except now I was able to hear what he was saying.

I didn't feel scared. I felt excited.

When I got home, I told Nate what was going on.

He shrugged. "I haven't heard of that happening before, but if it feels safe to you just go with it."

"I think he can leave if he wants to, he just doesn't want to yet. He can use his five senses again from inside my body. After being dead for over 600 years, I'm sure that's pretty great." I smiled, knowing the spirit could hear me.

The next day I made a point to go down to the Sanctuary to visit with the other spirits. I marched straight over to Skunk Man's grave pile and pointed to it.

"That's where you belong," I said. "Why don't you go back inside?"

I am in there. At least my body still is. What you're hearing isn't actually me, only my spirit.

I rolled my eyes. "I wasn't planning on being possessed," I muttered under my breath.

I walked over to the old chief's grave, the man whom I had started talking to first. I held out the rods in my hands awaiting an answer before I asked, "Don't you think Skunk Man should go back inside his grave and leave my head?"

Yes, that would be best.

I froze. I had heard his big, strong, booming voice inside my head. Just like I was hearing Skunk Man.

"How did you do that?!" I cried out loud.

Calm down, he replied. *You can hear me because the other is already here. We can all hear each other.*

"Great. Fucking great," I said and threw up my hands in

exasperation. "Now I'm possessed by two Native American medicine men. Anybody else want to join the party?"

I began pacing the graveyard, thinking about what I should do. On the one hand, I was incredibly excited and felt honored that they had chosen to communicate with me, of all people, even though I was a white person.

I had always shown respect for their culture and to them in the best way I knew how. I wanted to be one of them so badly I could feel it in my bones. But I knew I wasn't, so I had remained respectful and helpful when I could be.

I finally deduced that of course they would talk with me. Nobody else (besides Dan) had even tried to talk with them for the last 600+ years. I had shown up, cleaned all their graves, honored their existence, thanked them, and begun sitting at their historic ceremony site and using it for its original intent. Combine that with the fact that I was a practicing Herbalist and helping people heal as part of my business during that time, and I dared to hope that perhaps someday they might even call me a medicine woman.

No one else could hear their voices. They were only inside my head. They weren't exactly "audible" so much as the words and intonation simply appeared in my consciousness as if I was speaking with a man standing right in front of me. I couldn't ignore them any more than you could ignore a person physically standing right in front of you.

"Okay, okay," I said out loud again. "I'm just glad I can hear you too. Do either of you have a name?"

Skunk Man spoke first. I am called Kanakstaka.

Then the original spoke. I am Powono.

There are others here, but some may not want to speak with you, Powono said. And some are too old to speak anymore.

I nodded solemnly. After Powono had shown me all the grave sites it was no surprise; some were quite short and spread out, as if they had been piled so long ago that the earth was reclaiming them. I walked over to the grave of the old medicine woman and said hello.

She has no interest in telling you her name, Powono said. It was stated simply and not meant to offend, so I brushed it off and walked up the trail a bit further. I found another grave where I had placed a quartz stone and sat down on the ground beside it.

Hi! I nearly jumped when I heard the voice in my head. It was bouncy, jovial, and slightly wild. My name is Yahto. I'm so happy to be with you!

I smiled. "Hello, Yahto. You can call me Amelia."

Now I had three. I decided that was enough for one day,

so I gathered my bag and rods and headed back up the trail.

Close to the end, near the base of the field, my attention was brought to a huge boulder on my left. Scraggly vines grew around the base, and several large branches had fallen from the trees overhead and were scattered on top of it. There were some stones on top of the boulder, making it look like one giant grave pile. I picked my way around the vines and sticks at the base and crossed to the other side.

There is a spirit here too, Powono said. So, I climbed up on the boulder carefully and tossed the big branches down off it. I cleared a space from the top and sat there for a moment, fishing a piece of quartz from my pocket to lay on top of it.

"I honor your life," I said out loud. "You are not forgotten."

Thank you, said a woman's voice inside my head.

I smiled, not knowing if she could see me or just sense me. "I'm Amelia," I said. "What's your name?"

I had to listen for a minute or two. The birds chirped overhead and the breeze blew my hair. The sun was beginning to set for the afternoon, but it looked beautiful on the other side of the boulder beyond the trail. There was a small piece of land with grass waving in the breeze and some moss near the trees around the edge of the open space. The dappled sunlight hit the ground in a beautiful pattern. Suddenly, I heard her voice again.

That's my name, she said. Sunshine on the Meadow.

"That's a beautiful name!" I said. "May I call you Meadow for short?"

Yes. I could feel her smile.

So now I had four spirits talking to me.

"I need to head home now," I said. "But I'll be back tomorrow and we can talk again. Is that okay?"

Yes, they all said in agreement. See you tomorrow.

And so I left.

The following two weeks were a blur. I went to the farm to work my schedule, but I would also drive out to the property and immediately hit the trail so I could spend time with my new friends as often as possible. The spirits began visiting me while I worked, offering me conversation while I weeded, hauled mulch, or harvested beans.

I brought Marie and Ray to visit the Sanctuary, as they had not seen it yet. Through my psychic connection to the medicine men spirits, I was able to show them the graves and relay their words to the spirits. Ray surprised me by telling us that he channels messages from Sitting

Bull during his spirit ceremonies, though he did not choose to demonstrate while I was watching.

The companionship of the four spirits I regularly communed with did not end at the farm though. I was able to speak to them through some sort of psychic channel. Powono was teaching me life lessons from his people. Yahto was like a wild man of the woods who helped me identify new mushrooms and discover herbal medicines I had not heard of before. Meadow was like a steady hand of reason, giving me the confidence to be barefoot in the forest and fearless in any stretch of woods I entered.

And Kanakstaka was an incorrigible flirt. He had taken a fancy to me and wanted my attention above all others.

It was strange. I had feelings for him too, despite not being able to see him. I didn't feel like I was cheating on Nate because in all honesty, no one could see or hear Kanakstaka besides me. What was there to argue with?

Inside my mind, he had fallen in love with me. He kissed me when no one was looking. He demanded to have sex with me whether we were in the forest or in my own bed. And since in my mind's eye, he was far more attractive than my own depressed, miserable husband, I let it happen.

Of course, we weren't actually having sex. But when I was alone, I felt his invisible hands touching my skin. I would lay down (the floor, the grass, the sofa, just about anywhere) and my hips would gyrate up into the air as I wrapped my legs around an invisible force. He finished quickly, time and again, but I was used to that from every other man I'd been with. I was a vessel for his pleasure. It didn't matter. He wanted me and I wanted his attention.

Kanakstaka was tall and handsome with long black hair and red-gold skin. He wore a deer hide vest with his chest bared and a skunk skin over his shoulders. He was the most beautiful man I'd ever seen.

Over and over, I was far more satisfied by the man inside my own head than anything in the world around me. He became possessive after a while, demanding my attention more and more. Proving that he could please me sexually and that he was the best man for me.

I spent hours both in my yard and in the ceremony circle with my eyes both open and closed, desperately trying to see him and the others. When I closed my eyes, I could feel them beside me. I could see their faces, feel Kanakstaka's breath on my neck, smell the leather of Powono's medicine pouch that hung from a thong around his neck.

They were as real to me as you are to yourself. But I could not see them.

Eventually I told my kids that Mommy was able to talk with spirits. It helped them understand why they would sometimes see me speaking softly to no one in particular while I was out in my garden, or why I would get up at dawn and bang my drum in the backyard as the sun rose over the trees.

I collected a pile of white quartz boulders from Marie's farm and set them up in a small tower in my backyard. This was my new ritual place, and I would stand beside it to drum or sing whenever I wanted to feel more connected to my Native friends and their roots.

When they all showed up at my house that night, I was sure I had made a mistake. I'd thought their spirits could only be in the forest near their graves, but I could feel them here at my home. Powono told me that the quartz pile had created a conduit for their spirits to travel between the two places. I was surprised, but I accepted it as a good thing. Now my new friends could be even closer.

One evening Powono and Kanakstaka helped me communicate with the spirit of a dead boy who inhabited my basement. There was a place on the floor in my basement that, despite being a cement floor, sounded hollow underneath. I wasn't sure what could be under it, but it was creepy.

Powono and the dousing rods helped me discover that a little boy had wandered into the basement of my house when it was first being built and fallen into a deep hole. His friend, another boy from the neighborhood, had run away instead of telling anyone. And the following day the boy's body had been buried in the cement, never to be seen again. The hollow sound we heard when tapping on the floor was the crater that had sunk over time around where the boy's body had decomposed. He told us his name was Adam and he missed his parents. There wasn't much I could do to help him, but I said hello every time I went into the basement from that point on.

At one point during the week, I had gone back to the woods behind my house and sensed an evil presence there. Powono was with me, helping me prepare a spot on the big flat rock that Randy had mentioned during his reading so that it could be my new outdoor meditation place.

Feeling threatened, I called my friend Erin, who was an expert at helping spirits of all kinds pass from being stuck here on earth through to the spirit realm on the other side. She had been giving me advice on opening my pineal gland so that I could finally see my spirit friends, so we were in touch regularly.

She lived nearby and the following day she came to my house around lunchtime. As soon as she stepped into my kitchen, where the basement door was, she said "I sense a little boy here. Is your son home?"

Surprised, I told her no, he was at school. "There's a spirit of a boy in the basement, though," I said, hoping she didn't think I sounded nuts.

"Is his name Adam?" she asked.

My eyes grew wide and I exclaimed, "Yes! Holy crap, how did you know that?"

She smiled. "He just told me."

"Can you help him pass over to the other side?" I asked. "Not that he isn't a nice kid, but I'm sure he's sick of living in my basement for the last 70 years."

She followed me into the basement where I sat on the old beat-up couch we had down there and she chose a spot to stand that wasn't full of cobwebs. She pulled a crystal from her pocket that dangled on a thin chain and held it over her hand.

"Hi Adam," she said gently. Erin was shorter than me but pretty, with wide features and long blonde hair. She didn't have any children yet, but I could see her being a good mother someday.

"Would you like to go home to your mom and dad?" she asked. The crystal began to spin above her hand, slow at first and then more rapidly in a wide circle. "Good," she said with a smile.

She spoke a few more words and I watched in awe as the crystal spun wildly for a few moments and then suddenly stopped.

Just stopped. Hovering right over her palm. "He's gone," she said.

"Thank you!" I replied with relief. Now can we go get the asshole out in the woods?"

I walked her outside and through the backyard, all the way to the edge of the wooded area. She held the crystal out over her palm again and spoke into the forest. "Oh, I can feel you," she said to the empty woods. Her tone implied her displeasure.

"Yeah, he's a real asshole, whoever he was," I said. I could feel the evil presence mocking me.

"You're ready to leave this place," she commanded.

The pendulum swung back and forth vehemently. "Yes, you are," she replied, disagreeing with his negative response. It's time."

She spoke a few words and the pendulum swung in a circle, faster and faster. I could feel Kanakstaka's arms around me and I knew Powono's spirit stood in front of me, shielding me from any spiritual damage.

Suddenly, the crystal stopped spinning dead in its tracks. Erin breathed a deep sigh, then shook her hand off as if it was dirty. "He's gone," she said finally, stuffing the crystal back into her pocket.

I thanked her. She turned back and came closer to me. "What's going on with you?" she asked curiously.

So, I told her about the spirits and the Native Ceremony

circle and the graves. "They're with me all the time," I said. "Even now."

She smiled, looking at me thoughtfully. "I can feel them around you," she said. "You are very loved and protected right now."

I smiled back, patting my left shoulder where I knew Kanakstaka's hand was on me. "I know," I said.

I thanked her again for her help and she went home for the day.

One night I started drinking a bottle of mead that I had made and Kanakstaka told me, "Drink more. If you drink enough, you can see us!"

I drank the entire bottle. I went outside in the dark, staring up at the stars in the night sky. I still couldn't see him. "Drink more, try harder!" He said.

I stumbled back into the house and took a shot of straight bourbon.

Nate was beginning to get concerned. "They told me I could see them if I was drunk," I explained. He seemed hesitant but kept an eye on me.

I went out into the backyard again. Spin! Spin fast and get dizzy. Then open your eyes. We are here!

Yahto egged him on, encouraging me to get dizzy. I spun around in circles, becoming woozy from all the alcohol in my system. When I opened my eyes, all I saw was the dark world of my backyard around me.

I threw up. Nate helped me back into the house and I put myself to bed. Kanakstaka and Yahto laid in bed with me, apologetic. "We thought it would work," they both said.

I knew they were there for me. I was more upset that I couldn't see them the way I wanted to than that I'd gotten myself nearly blackout drunk trying. I fell asleep in Kanakstaka's arms, reveling in his breath on my shoulder and feeling safe again.

Two days later I went to the same park where I had seen the white owl and ran into Randy the shaman. "Hi!" I said excitedly.

As usual for him, he greeted me but looked slightly nervous. He was there with his girlfriend, an older woman with bedraggled blonde-gray hair who wore a woolen poncho and a perpetually dismal expression on her face.

I told Randy all about the Native graveyard and how the spirits of the medicine men were talking with me, and I had given them offerings.

"This must be what it's like when you talk with the spirits, right?" I asked.

He looked at me like a deer in the headlights. "Yeah, of course, though I don't hear actual voices. More like images. The spirit world can be very dangerous."

I agreed. "I'm quite protected, so I'm not concerned about that. They make me feel very safe." I could feel Kanakstaka bristling; if he was there in body rather than just spirit, he would have been standing tall and menacing, even though Randy was clearly no threat to him.

"I discovered a Native grave spot the last time I was here a few weeks ago," I told Randy. He is an old spirit and said his name is Wakapoti."

"Oh yeah," Randy said, giving me a fake smile. "Yeah, Wakapoti, I know. Nice guy." He gathered his things and his girlfriend. "We better get going now," he said.

I shrugged and offered him a quick hug. "Thank you for believing in me," I said. Don't be a stranger!"

He nodded pleasantly before he got into his car and left.

What an odd guy, I thought. It's almost like he doesn't believe me. But he's doing the same thing so I don't know how that could be.

I don't like him, Kanakstaka said.

"You don't like anybody dear," I replied with a playful smile. We went on our short hike in the woods and after a while, went home.

I visited my friends a few days later. I told Dan and Ann what had happened at the Sanctuary—how I had accidentally invited one of the medicine men's spirits to inhabit my body and that now I was able to hear and communicate with them.

Dan looked at me with trepidation. "You'd better be careful, Amelia. That's a dangerous thing to do."

I nodded. "I know it sounds scary, but they don't seem to be hurting me at all. Just talking to me."

Ann shrugged, clearly a bit worried for me. "If I were you, I'd demand they leave you alone and go back to their resting place," she said. "You don't need another spirit attached to your physical body."

I could feel Kanakstaka bristle when she said that. I squeezed my own leg in reassurance, letting him know it was safe. "I understand. I'm going to do that soon," I lied.

The truth was, with the spirits in my mind talking to me and offering me love and support, I felt less alone. Like someone finally understood me and was giving me what I needed emotionally, rather than my having to fight for what I wanted and convince them that I was worthy of it.

I left Dan and Ann that day with the assurance that I

would be fine and could control whether the spirits talked with me or not.

I had no idea how wrong I was.

The following week, my 38th birthday was on Tuesday and Friday was a big day for us. Nate's father had planned a trip out from Wisconsin to visit us, and we'd been making plans for where to take him and what to do, since we'd have the kids that weekend.

I celebrated my birthday without incident, eating a cheesecake that Nate brought home from the store for me and spending as much time as I wanted in the forest with my closest friends, the ones only I could hear.

On Thursday afternoon, Nate came home early to help prepare for the next few days off visiting with his father. I'd gotten the kids home from school and they were playing inside the house while I dug in the garden harvesting my ginger and turmeric crop. The sun was shining brightly, the air holding that late-summer magic of being warm in the sun yet extra cool in the shade, and I was happily getting my crop in while my Indigenous friends watched.

I was conversing pleasantly with them as I loosened the soil to pull the ginger rhizomes up when Yahto dropped a bomb on me: while he was alive, he had raped several women.

I stared at the empty spot of air where I thought his face must be and gave him a disapproving glare. "That's a terrible thing to do," I said. "I don't think I want you around me anymore."

I haven't done it in a long time though, he whined. I could feel Kanakstaka step up beside me protectively.

"Still," I said. "That isn't good. You were not a good man, Yahto. I don't want you around me anymore."

He was hurt and angry. He stomped away, glaring at me from beside the pile of quartz rocks up near the back porch. I lifted up the two buckets full of ginger and turmeric and began hauling them out of the garden back towards the house. I brought the buckets into the kitchen and set them down.

Nate came up to me to see the harvest. "The kids are upstairs in Gabe's room," he said. "Wow, we got a lot of ginger this year!"

I nodded, then crossed my arms and leaned back against the kitchen counter, glaring angrily at an empty spot of air on the opposite side of the kitchen.

"What is it?" Nate asked.

"Yahto is a rapist," I said in a cold, judgmental tone. "I don't think I want him around me anymore. But he doesn't want to leave."

None of us will leave you, Kanakstaka said.

Uncovering *Amy*

I stood up straight. I didn't like the tone of his voice. "What do you mean?" I asked nervously. "I think you should all go home now."

Nate walked back to the living room to allow me time to talk with my friends, knowing he couldn't understand them.

We're never leaving you. *I'm* never leaving you.

I thought carefully for a moment. In an instant, the whole charade washed away. My voice quavered as I asked, "How many of you are there here?"

I could feel him smile. One.

"One?! What do you mean one?"

It's always only been one. I am here. And I'm not leaving.

"Nate?" I called into the other room. He came out to me.

"I'm getting scared," I said, clearly shaken. "I just found out that there's only one of them. There's only been one spirit this whole time."

His eyebrows rose. "What does that mean?"

"I'm not sure, but he said he wasn't leaving."

I felt as if the spirit had placed his arms around me lovingly, as Kanakstaka used to do. "Go away," I growled under my breath. "I need time alone!"

No.

I ignored him. I heard the kids coming down the stairs and I needed to cook dinner for everyone.

Somehow, I managed to turn off the noise inside my head and make dinner, putting their needs above my own for a couple of hours. We ate and got them set up in front of the TV for a movie after dinner was finished.

Kanakstaka had created a short song to sing to me a week earlier, telling me how much he loved me in his own language. He wouldn't stop singing it in my ear now.

"Go away," I demanded quietly, trying not to frighten my family.

Never.

I managed to make it through the evening, I'm not sure how, and after I put the kids to bed, I crawled into bed with Nate. Kanakstaka would not stop singing.

Love me, he urged. I ignored him.

Eventually, after midnight, after I had lain in bed struggling to ignore him, I fell asleep.

<u>Friday, October 1st</u>

The next morning, I got the kids off to school and then Nate and I drove to the airport to pick his father up from his flight. Friday was happening so fast—I did my best to ignore the insistent voice inside my head, begging for attention. He sang, he pleaded, he gripped my leg using my own left (non-dominant) hand.

I told him to shut up. I focused on the road. We got Nate's dad and I was able to be my normal pleasant self for a while, ignoring any insistence from the masculine voice begging me for attention. We took him out for lunch at a great pizza place near our house.

Talk to me!!! The voice urged. I love you! Love me!

"Shut up! Why should I talk to you?" I asked it quietly, as soon as I'd gotten up to go to the bathroom.

Because we love each other! I need you! Love me again! Talk to me!

"I don't even know who you are anymore," I said.

I noticed around that time that it hurt when I urinated. I was not drinking enough water, and the voice was barely leaving me alone enough to take a few bites of food. I was beginning to feel physically sick, but I pushed through the day as if nothing was wrong to save face with my father-in-law.

After we finished lunch, I dropped Nate and his father off at the house and went to pick the kids up from school. Still ignoring the voice as best I could, I had a thought.

The quartz stones! Perhaps if I removed those offerings from the graves of the medicine people it would break the connection they had with me.

After I got back home and sent the kids in for a snack, I grabbed the big white quartz boulders from the pile and dismantled it. I threw them up against the back porch, rolling this way and that. Then I brought a homemade smudge stick (a bundle of sage, mugwort, and other herbs that I could light for aromatic smoke and prayer purposes) and lit it, waving the smoke all over my back-yard with a big feather.

"We have to go remove the offering stones!" I told Nate insistently. "I think that's the only way to get him out of our house."

Nate said "Okay," but then looked at me with a funny expression on his face.

"You can go ahead but it's not going to work." I froze. The words had come out of my mouth, but I had not spoken them.

"That wasn't me!" I squeaked in a panic. I didn't say that just now!" My eyes were round with fear.

It was already 4pm, but this was an emergency. Nate

asked his dad if he could watch the kids and the two of us hopped into my truck and raced back to the farm.

Nate followed me around the forest, climbing through underbrush and up over big stones, holding a plastic bag for me while I collected all the quartz stones that I had placed on every grave I could find. Every single offering that I'd left … I took back.

"This isn't going to help you," my own voice said to me, making a mocking face.

MY OWN FACE had crinkled up. Then it laughed at me. With my own voice.

The spirit was no longer only in my head. It wasn't just a voice or feeling that only I could hear. It had taken control of my body.

I was in a panic. Nate was even getting freaked out.

"Ha, ha, you can't stop me!" it said in a sing-song voice.

I grabbed another handful of white quartz. "Oh no, not that!" it said through my mouth, mocking me.

After an hour we had finally collected all the stones, then we hopped into the truck and sped home.

I managed to make dinner and pretend like everything was normal in front of Nate's father. But inside, the voice was singing the song that Kanakstaka had made up for me. My left hand (my non-dominant hand) was held with the pointer finger out, circling over and over on my thigh. So even though it was silent with my voice, I knew it was there.

I did my best not to panic. I thought I could control it somewhat. I desperately didn't want to scare my kids.

I called Marie and left a voicemail begging for her help. She wasn't home. So, I called Erin.

Erin told me over the phone that she could sense evil spirits inhabiting me. "I'm trying to pull them out, but I can only do so much from over here," she said. I could hear the fear in her voice, but I could also tell that she was doing her best to help. "I've pulled out 17 so far, but more keep showing up! Can you get over here tonight?"

"No no no!" the voice said through my own gritted teeth.

"Sorry, that was the spirit Erin," I apologized. "Yes, I'll get over there right away."

"You can't get rid of me," it hissed with my own mouth. I could feel my own face contorting into an expression of anger when it spoke with my voice.

"Like hell I can't!" I replied angrily.

I told Nate where I was going and instructed him to watch the kids.

It was time to end this bullshit.

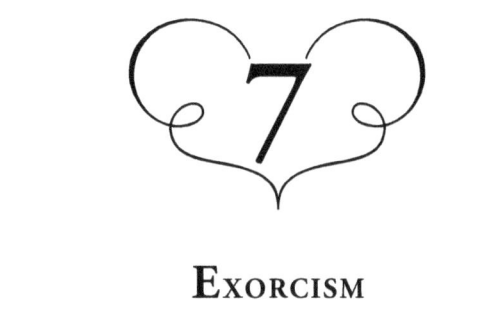

7

Exorcism

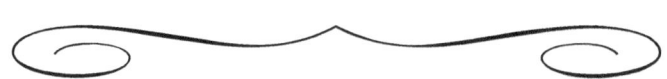

I grabbed my rattle and drum and popped into the truck to drive the ten minutes to Erin's house. The voice would stop talking and give me a break when I shook the rattle, so I did my best to shake it with one hand and drive with the other, all whilst trying desperately to swallow the rising sense of panic I was feeling.

When I arrived, I stepped out of the truck and looked up at the stars in the night sky. "Please help me, God," I said softly with tears in my eyes. I didn't care which god answered, only that someone, somewhere, could help me get through this.

My own mouth curled into a sneer and chuckled. "Not gonna happen," he said.

I left my rattle in the vehicle and walked up the sidewalk. Erin opened the door seconds after I knocked.

"I need help!" I said, barely able to hold back my tears. "Whatever this thing is inside me I want it OUT!"

"I got you, it's okay," she said soothingly. Her dog walked up to me, wagging his tail happily and I patted him on the head. "Here, lay down on the couch," she gestured to her black sofa, just a few feet from the door.

I sat down, then lay back on the sofa with my head propped on a pillow on one side. She offered me a glass of water, which I thanked her for even though I could barely take a few sips. I set the glass on her coffee table and looked up at her large screen television across the other side of the room. She clicked a few buttons on her remote control and turned on a soothing nature station: just nature scenes with soft music accompaniment. She lit a few candles and suggested I try to relax.

"It's hard to relax when my mouth is talking on its own," I said with a shaky voice.

My own voice, lower and growling, snarled "YOU'RE NOT GETTING RID OF ME!"

"Fuck you!" I yelled at myself. "I don't want you here anymore! Get the fuck out!"

Erin's eyes grew wide. Her boyfriend came out from a room down the hall with a large book in his hand. She looked at him.

"I think this is a demon," she said. She pulled her crystal on a chain from her pocket and held it out over my body. It began spinning wildly almost immediately.

She used her opposite hand and made pulling gestures,

 Uncovering *Amy*

as if she was removing long strands of something from my body that I couldn't physically see.

"You're getting out of her, guy, I don't care what you say," Erin said with confidence as she worked over my body. "Are you a Christian Demon?" she asked.

"Fuck you!" my mouth screamed at her.

"Start looking up Christian demons, babe," Erin called to her boyfriend. He opened the large volume on the kitchen counter where he stood.

"I'm going to say letters and you're going to tell me which letter your name starts with." Erin said to me, speaking to the demon.

She held her crystal over me again, asking yes or no questions. "A ... B ... C ... D ... E ... F ... G ... yes? G?" She turned her head again. "Look under G, babe!" she said to her boyfriend.

He began reading off demon names that started with the letter G. My body twisted and my mouth screamed a loud, angry cry. "Gamigin? That's you?" My mouth growled and yelled again. "Gotcha, fucker," she said with a smile.

"Fuck you! You can fuck off!" My mouth let out a string of angry profanities at her, followed by growls and screams. The demon did not want anyone to know its name.

Erin grabbed another book off her shelf and opened it to a page. I vaguely recognized it as a Christian bible. She began reciting The Lord's Prayer at me.

My body writhed and screamed again. When she finished, I took a breath. It seemed like the demon had calmed down.

She took a deep breath. "Fight fire with fire," she said with a smile. "How do you feel?"

My body was shaking. "He isn't gone," I said weakly. "I think he just doesn't want to scream anymore right now."

"I'm not going anywhere," my own voice said again, low and threatening.

Erin sat down beside me just as I was sitting up on the sofa. "Can you get hold of my friend Marie?" I asked. "She can take me to someone who can help, I think." She nodded and grabbed her cell phone, which had better signal than mine.

Only ten minutes later, a knock came at the door.

"Is Amelia okay?" Marie asked as Erin let her in.

"I'm not dead yet," I said with a smile.

My head quickly twisted to the side, and I could feel my lip curl. "Yet," he repeated.

Marie's eyes grew wide. Erin told her what had happened. "I'll take Amelia's truck back to her house; Dave can just follow me and bring me home. Can you help her?" Erin said, grabbing my car keys from my purse on the kitchen counter.

Marie nodded, helping me up off the couch.

"Take me to Dan, he's the only one who can help me!" I said. "I don't think anyone else knows how to speak with this kind of spirit."

"Of course, I already called them to tell them we're on our way. Ann said he isn't feeling well but they said they can talk to you." Marie led me out to her car, and I thanked Erin before she drove off in my truck to bring it home for me.

"I can't control it, Marie. Erin said it's a demon inside me. I'm wondering if it's a Wendigo.[4] Either way I want it out." I was still shaking as I talked to her. She drove as fast as she dared; it was already nearing 9pm and the roads were dark and bare.

"We're going to get this fixed, it will be okay," she told me while watching the road. I was grateful for her reassurance, but I could hear the fear and uncertainty in her voice. I said nothing and rode in silence, my hands gripping my thighs like claws to keep the beast inside me quiet.

We rolled up to Dan's house just as he and Ann were

walking out the door to meet us. Dan looked ill: sweaty, red-faced, and tired. But he was there for me and I was grateful. We both stepped out and walked to the end of the ramp that led to the front door. Ann held her hand up to stop us.

"We don't want you inside," she said. I couldn't see her face very well as we only had the distant streetlights down the road and the single light above their garage door to see by, but she seemed scared.

"I'm possessed by a demon," I said to her simply.

"HA! You can't stop me!" My own voice yelled at them wildly. I gritted my teeth, hoping to keep it silent. My left foot stomped angrily on the pavement and Marie held my arm to keep me from throwing my body to the ground.

"We told you that you shouldn't have let them inside you," Dan said.

"This is because of all that pagan stuff you do," Ann added. "You can't get rid of this unless you accept Jesus Christ as your savior." Dan nodded in agreement.

My brow furrowed. This was the first time either of them had mentioned anything about Christianity so I was confused where this sudden piety had come from. I was silent for a moment, internally disagreeing. I didn't think this had anything to do with me not being a Christian. If a demon can possess someone, what difference did it make what religious beliefs that person had?

"Can't you do anything to help me get it out?" I pleaded, directing my eyes at Dan.

He seemed weak, and I could tell he was sick, but his conviction was strong. "I haven't got the strength to fight something like this right now," he said.

"Tomorrow?" I asked.

He shook his head. "There's nothing I can do for you. I suggest you call the church in the morning and see if they can help you."

I thought for a moment. "This thing is barely letting me eat or drink," I said. "And I think I have a urinary tract infection now too."

Ann went back inside the house for a moment. She emerged again with a bottle of Ocean Spray cranberry juice and a book about Feminine Christian Divine Power. She handed them both to me. "This will help you," she said.

I nodded. Marie and I thanked them both and went back to her car.

"I don't know what to do," I said in a shaky voice as she drove me back to my house. "I haven't been sleeping. This thing won't leave me alone."

"I'm going to call a few places first thing in the morning

and see if I can get you some help from the church," she said reassuringly. "We'll get this thing out of you, don't worry."

She pulled into my driveway and I saw my truck there, having been delivered by Erin. "I hope I get some sleep tonight," I said as I stood up to get out of her car.

"I'll call you in the morning," she said.

I went inside the house. Nate was sitting on the couch with his dad; a beer casually held in both their hands.

"I put the kids to bed," he assured me. I thanked him and checked on my children in each of their rooms. They were safe and sound, asleep in their beds. I felt guilty for not being there to sing them to sleep as I normally did, but this was an emergency.

I walked upstairs to change out of my clothes and get into pajamas. "You better not harm my kids, you bastard," I said quietly to the thing inside my head.

I would never hurt the kids, it said inside my head. That surprised me. I was tired, so tired.

I brushed my teeth and crawled into bed, not waiting for Nate to join me. I lay there, curled on my side. The voice sang to me, the sweet song of love that it had come up with when it was pretending to be Kanakstaka. I couldn't stand it.

It would not let me sleep.

I lay there silently in bed, singing "Hakuna Matata" from The Lion King movie repeatedly as loudly as my conscious mind could manage. Eventually, Nate joined me. And sometime after 2am, I finally passed out.

<u>Saturday morning October 2nd</u>

I woke up late, but I managed to get up and cook breakfast for my family.

The thing was still there. As soon as I was conscious, it started telling me how much it loved me and how it wanted to stay. I managed to ignore it long enough to eat some scrambled eggs, but I still couldn't seem to get enough water in me. I felt dehydrated and tired. I put a strong face on in front of my kids, but inside I was starting to wonder how long I would have to deal with this.

I didn't think I could handle it much longer.

I began texting and emailing people. Friends, family, whoever I thought might support me in some way. I emailed Wendy and Rick telling them I'd been possessed, I sent an email to Randy begging him to help me get the Wendigo out of my body, and I asked my parents to pray for me.

I didn't live close to much of my family, and part of me was embarrassed to ask for their help. Every friend I had, I asked to send prayers and healing energy my way.

Around 10am, Marie called me on my cell and told me she had been making phone calls all morning and managed to get me help from a priest after the 12pm service at St. James Catholic Church.

I felt relief wash over me, followed by a wave of fear from the spirit inside. Then it started laughing at me.

This thing had control over my emotions from a certain perspective. I thought I could feel help coming to me from prayers of other metaphysical spiritualists that I knew along with all my friends, and I felt joy at the thought that a priest could certainly pull this evil spirit from my body.

But this thing could only give me fleeting sensations. A wave of fear, followed by a wave of mocking laughter. I didn't know what was real or what was me anymore.

Thankfully, my father-in-law was having a good time playing with and watching my kids for me while Nate stood by, concerned about me but not really knowing how to help. I told him that Marie was going to help me at the church.

Nate took his father aside while the kids were coloring in the living room and quietly told him what was going on. To his credit, he didn't just demand I get sent off to the Looney Bin but instead wanted to help however he could. Nate asked him to watch the kids so he could accompany me to the church with Marie.

My phone rang around 11am, after I'd been texting and messaging people all morning to ask for help, and my dad, who lived in Georgia, was on the other end of the line.

"I'm possessed by a demon," I told him with a quavering voice. "My friend tried to pull it out, but she couldn't. My other friend is taking me to the church in an hour. I've barely slept and hardly eaten or drank anything since Thursday."

"I think I know someone who can help you," he said. "Is it okay if I give him your phone number and he calls you as soon as he can?"

At this point I was willing to accept help from the Stay Puft Marshmallow Man if I thought it would work, so of course I told him yes. I was open to anyone or anything that could help me get rid of this demon inside me.

Around 11:30, Marie came over and loaded me into her car, with Nate in the backseat. We drove over to the church and got out into the parking lot.

I had been raised a Catholic and knew Catholic church and how it worked well. The demon inside me wanted no part in it.

My throat rumbled with a deep growl. Marie took my left side, and Nate held my arm on the right. They led me up the stairs into the back of the church. I hissed when we walked through the door and moaned in pain when Marie put holy water on my forehead.

Other parishioners looked sideways at me as we walked in and took a spot in a pew on the left-hand side, not near the front but close enough that the priest could see me. He had been warned ahead of time. The church was large inside but only maybe 25 people had shown up for Saturday Mass.

The priest started his presentation. I stood there with Marie and Nate holding me on either side. I was able to control my body enough to sit and stand as the priest asked everyone to do. He spoke a brief sermon about the devil, quoting:

Ephesians 6:10–13

"Finally, be strong in the Lord and in the strength of his might. Put on the whole armor of God, that you may be able to stand against the schemes of the devil. For we do not wrestle against flesh and blood, but against the rulers, against the authorities, against the cosmic powers over this present darkness, against the spiritual forces of evil in the heavenly places. Therefore, take up the whole armor of God, that you may be able to withstand in the evil day, and having done all, to stand firm."

While the priest spoke, he looked me straight in the eyes from his place standing at the Holy Table. My face whipped to the side and a low, long growl escaped my throat. My left foot stamped hard on the floor, and a grimace covered my face.

The parishioners closest to me gave me sideways glances, wondering what the heck was going on. I tried to force myself to stare ahead at the altar. The priest offered Communion, but I refused. I knew that would be a very bad idea in my state.

About half an hour later, the priest ended the service. I saw both him and his helper look my way as they left the chancel and went back behind the curtain. We stood in the pew and waited for everyone else to leave.

After a few minutes, the priest came back out and walked over to us. Marie and Nate led me out from the pew, and we followed them to a back room of the church.

The priest laid his hand on my forehead and began reciting the exorcism prayer.

"In the Name and by the power of Our Lord Jesus Christ, may you be snatched away and driven from the Church of God and from the souls made to the image and likeness of God and redeemed by the Precious Blood of the Divine Lamb. The Most High God commands you, He with whom, in your great insolence, you still claim to be equal.

"Stoop beneath the all-powerful Hand of God; tremble and flee when we invoke the Holy and terrible Name of

Jesus, this Name which causes hell to tremble, this Name to which the Virtues, Powers and Dominations of heaven are humbly submissive, this Name which the Cherubim and Seraphim praise unceasingly repeating: Holy, Holy, Holy is the Lord, the God of Hosts."

As he spoke, I screamed.

Screamed with bunched fists, my face looking up toward the ceiling, skin red hot with rage.

When he finally stopped, I looked him in the eyes, panting. After I caught my breath, I felt my face open into a wide grin.

"Better luck next time," the voice said through my mouth.

I started to cry. I still had barely eaten or drank all day, but I used their private bathroom while Nate and Marie asked the priest what to do next.

As I was coming out, the priest told her, "There isn't any more we can do. Maybe call the church in Norwich. They're the next biggest Catholic church in the area."

Marie nodded. They walked me outside again.

"You'll never get me out of here alive!" my voice said harshly.

I was sick of this shit. I walked right up to the outside of the church and placed both my hands on it.

My head flung back, mouth open, and a blood-curdling scream left my throat. I stepped away after taking a breath. "Take that motherfucker," I said to the demon inside me.

It laughed.

The priest and his helper stared at me for a minute, shook their heads, and went back inside the church, closing the door behind them.

I thought about where else I could get help. Who can I pray to? Who do I know in the spirit realm that might fight for me?

My ancestors.

"Grandma, Grandpa, help me!" I yelled up at the sky. Then I touched the church again. The demon let out a scream, but I could feel my grandparents there (all four of them) helping me, giving me the strength to fight this thing.

Marie and Nate had had enough of me screaming outside the church. People were walking by and staring at us. They loaded me back into Marie's car and drove back to our house.

I logged into my old Ancestry.com account on my phone and renewed my subscription. I pulled up a list of my ancestors that I'd spent years discovering and cultivating. Once we got home, I ran into my house and printed the list out so I could hold it in my hand.

"Get the drums," I heard her telling Nate. "I've got Ray on his way over. We're going to get this thing out ourselves."

Nate gathered all the drums we had in the house. My kids didn't really know what was happening, but I told them: a demon is inside Mommy, and we need to get it out.

They were scared. My daughter was 12 and my son was 9. They had no understanding of the spirit realm, but they knew that mom was in pain and they were there to help. Nate handed each of them a drum and told them to start pounding on it. "Say 'get out of my mom!' Over and over, okay guys?" he told them.

They sat outside and did as they were told. I stood up against the outside of my house. I yelled the name of each one of my ancestors up into the sky, begging them to help me get rid of this demon inside me.

With each name I read, I felt stronger. My foot would stomp, as if they had arrived and were there behind me holding onto me.

"Get the fuck out of me, you bastard!" I yelled at myself.

Ray showed up and he brought two more drums. Marie held my shoulders and guided me carefully to the middle of the backyard. She handed me my drum, the one I had made myself, and I started banging on it with everything I had in me.

Nate and his father were there. The kids sat beside the garage on the ground, banging on their drums. Marie banged on hers and Ray his. Nate held me from behind to keep me steady and his father burned sage, using a feather to smudge[5] my body and everyone in the circle around me as we all prayed and begged the demon to leave.

I looked over at my kids. How could I do this to them? They didn't understand what was going on, all they knew was that Mommy was screaming in pain and they needed to beat their drums to help. I felt so guilty and helpless.

This went on for hours.

All I can remember now is the constant drumming. My drum, two drums on either side of me, my kids off to the side drumming inconsistently but frequently. And tears streaming down my face.

"Help me, God!" I cried over and over. "Yes, there's one, not many! I'm begging you, please help me get rid of this demon!"

By the second hour, Marie decided we needed help. She called a friend of hers, Rachel, whom I had never met before, but who had experience cleansing homes spiritually. Rachel arrived a short time later and smudged the entire inside of our house.

She came outside when she was finished and blew sage

smoke at all of us. We had been drumming for well over two hours at that point. I felt like my arm was going to fall off.

She placed her hand on my shoulder. "You can do this," she said encouragingly to me.

I had never met this woman before, and my eyes had been closed as I looked up at the sky. I could see the sun beginning to set from behind my eyelids. I just knew there was a helpful hand on my shoulder and a friendly voice beside me.

"You can leave her now. Go into the light! It's safe to leave her now." Rachel said soothingly, speaking to the demon.

"Light?" it said in a gravelly, dry voice.

"Yes, go into the light," she repeated.

My face looked up. "Liiiiiight…." My face said slowly. I could tell the spirit was as tired as I felt. But it was still inside me. It had to go.

"Step into the light."

"Okay. One foot," said the voice through my mouth.

"Yes, then the next," she said.

"Another foot," said the voice.

"And another foot. And another."

"How many feet do you have? I asked it."

"Seven. Plus tail. Too much to go into light," it said.

Oh now you're just fucking with me, I thought angrily.

Rachel wasn't deterred. "Step into the light. It's safe. Just go."

"You can do this baby, You're so strong! Go into the light," Nate was crying while holding me from behind, begging the gods to take this evil demon from my body.

"Liiiiiiiight," it said softly.

After a few more minutes, when the sun was no longer up in the sky and shade had begun to cover the yard, there was some blessed silence.

I stopped drumming. Everyone did. My father-in-law had brought the kids inside to get some food. Nate looked at me with tears in his eyes.

"Is it gone?" he asked.

"No." it replied.

We all shuddered. Shoulders sank. We had tried so hard!

"You're not a demon, are you?" Rachel asked me then. I noticed her for the first time now that my eyes were open. Short, plump, in her early 60s, with gray-blonde curly hair. She had kind eyes and was very patient with me.

My mouth turned into a grin. "No," the voice said through my mouth.

She stood there, opening her senses, and said "I can see spirits. You're a man."

My face grinned again and nodded.

"I see him in a uniform from the Revolutionary War," she explained. "His name was Robert. He was very handsome in that uniform!"

The spirit inside me smiled smugly. "Thank you," he said.

Rachel continued. "He was a soldier during King Philip's War. He killed a lot of Native Americans."

Ray came closer. Being of Cherokee descent, he decided to offer a feather of peace. "I will forgive you on behalf of my tribe," he said to the spirit inside me known as Robert.

"I feel like he was an ancestor to someone here," Rachel said. She pulled out her cell phone and went to Google.

"See here!" she cried excitedly, showing me her phone screen. Robert Jones, King Philips War the screen said, beneath a photo from the 18th century. Even though the War[6] had been in the 17th century, the website was using a random photo of a soldier to get attention. It didn't matter—my ghost had a name. And apparently, he was upset that he had killed so many Native Americans during the war.

"Robert, will you leave Amelia alone?" Rachel asked me nicely.

"No," Robert replied. My head shook.

"Can we at least eat some dinner?" I asked the voice.

Silence for a moment. "Yes. I'm hungry."

Ray held his arm around me. "It's safe to leave now. You are forgiven for your crimes against my people," he said.

"Okay," Robert replied.

I wondered if it would work since Ray was Cherokee but the tribes that were killed in that war were Northeastern tribes, but I didn't press the matter. The important thing was that a native descendant was offering forgiveness to a soldier who killed native peoples. That was enough.

"We have to get going," Marie said finally. "We're both tired." Ray agreed with her.

Rachel wrote her phone number down on a piece of paper. When she handed it to me, she looked me straight in the eyes, speaking to Robert. "It's safe to leave this body now. You can pass over."

Robert looked back at her through my eyes and nodded

solemnly. She pressed my hands with hers, gave me another smile, and left.

Late as it was, I still managed to help Nate make dinner. We gathered around the table to eat and I thanked my kids, giving them both a strong hug. They seemed to be reassured by my acting more normal, and we were able to eat dinner in peace.

I could feel him inside me. Restless. But as tired as I felt from fighting all day, I could do nothing about it except ask him quietly to leave me alone.

Later that night, after I put the kids to bed, I had a thought. Could it be that Robert was one of my Spirit Guides? A benevolent spirit sent by the Universe to help me discover myself and my spiritual powers?

I called my friend Tim, a friend from my drum circles and one of the only people I had not yet asked for help, as he knew ways to connect to spirit guides and was familiar with the power of drumming.

"How would I know if this thing inside me is actually my spirit guide?" I asked him over the phone while I lay down on my bed, staring up at the ceiling.

"Spirit guides come when you need them to," he said kindly. "They also leave when you want them to. If this thing refuses to leave when you tell it to go away, I can't imagine it's benevolent. It's more likely got sinister intentions."

  Uncovering *Amy*

I sighed. "Okay, thank you."

"You going to be okay?" he asked.

"I hope so."

Then I called Rachel again. She sounded tired but wanted to help. "Robert, we asked you to go into the light," she said to the spirit inside me. "It's time to relax and let go."

I lay down on my bed again and let her speak softly, slowly, relaxing Robert to the point where I could barely feel him anymore.

"Thank you," I told her. "I appreciate all your help."

I set my phone down. "I want you to leave. Even if you're a good spirit I don't want you here anymore. Understand?" I was talking to myself.

Nothing. I felt nothing. Was he finally gone?

I went to the bathroom and looked at my reflection in the mirror. "I need you to leave me alone. Will you go away now?"

My own eyes stared back at me, the expression in them changing slightly from exhaustion to determination. My head turned ever so slightly to the left, then to the right.

No. I won't go.

I heaved a huge sigh. I had tried my best.

I got into my pajamas and crawled into bed. The voice sang to me, lightly and softly, but demanding my attention, nonetheless. I sang back at it as hard as I could, Hakuna Matata, what a wonderful phrase…

Eventually, after midnight, I just barely fell into some kind of sleep.

DIAGNOSE ME

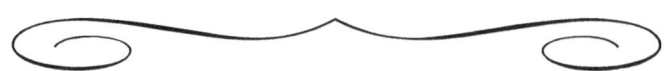

G o ahead, give it your best shot.

Whether you're a psychologist, psychiatrist, doctor of any kind, or just some regular person off the street, what would you think? If a woman with my symptoms was presented to you: insomnia, hearing voices, delusional, feeling things that aren't there, screaming as if possessed.

Would you lock me up in a strait jacket? Offer me some kind of anti-psychotic medication? Make me the center of some kind of soul retrieval ceremony? Send me to a bigger, better church to be tied down to a bed and exorcised by a team of priests?

I was desperate. I was at my wit's end. I had barely slept in three days, not drank enough water, barely ate, and was only keeping some semblance of sanity together for the sake of my kids and my visiting father-in-law.

Schizophrenia

A psychotic disorder characterized by disturbances in thinking (cognition), emotional responsiveness, and behavior, with an age of onset typically between the late teens and mid-30s.

The characteristic disturbances must last for at least 6 months and include at least 1 month of active-phase symptoms comprising two or more of the following: delusions, hallucinations, disorganized speech, grossly disorganized or catatonic behavior, or negative symptoms (e.g., lack of emotional responsiveness, extreme apathy).

Adapted from the APA Dictionary of Psychology[7]

Dissociative Identity Disorder (DID)

A dissociative disorder characterized by the presence in one individual of two or more distinct identities or personality states that each recurrently take control of the individual's behavior. It is believed to be associated with severe physical and sexual abuse, especially during childhood. Despite an increase in reported cases in the United States since the 1970s, DID remains the subject of considerable controversy, with many disputing its validity as a diagnosis and citing the incidences of childhood abuse reported by diagnosed individuals or their therapists as cases of false memory. DID is still commonly known as multiple personality disorder, a coinage usually attributed to U.S. physician Morton Prince

Uncovering *Amy*

(1854–1929), whose case history of his patient "Miss Beauchamp" (with personalities called Christine, Sally, and "the Idiot," among other names) was one of the first in-depth examinations of the phenomenon, published in The Dissociation of Personality in 1906. Subsequent case histories, especially the books The Three Faces of Eve (1957) and Sybil (1973) and their film adaptations, contributed to popularizing—some say sensationalizing—the phenomenon during the late 20th century. See also split personality.[8]

Split Personality

A lay term for an individual with dissociative identity disorder. It is sometimes confused with schizophrenia, which literally means "splitting of the mind," but does not involve the formation of a second personality.[9]

Demonic Possession[10]

This term describes a variety of conditions, both physical and emotional-mental-psychological, for which the cause is identified as direct demonic influence. The remedy that was used by Jesus and the Early Church for such conditions was exorcism.

So, which is it? Any of the above?

The fact is that I never got officially diagnosed with anything.

Stop and Think

If you were me, what would you have done?

Your body is exhausted. A voice inside your head that no one else can hear will not stop talking and singing to you and refuses to leave you a moment's peace. You've begged for help from every source you had available to you that wouldn't put you in a strait jacket. You just went through seven grueling hours of two separate exorcism rituals that did not solve your problem.

You have limited funds and you're supposed to go to work on Monday. You can't survive without working because you live paycheck to paycheck with virtually no savings. You have no history of psychological treatment or therapy because you never needed it before. And you don't want to lose your kids.

You're barely sleeping. You're fighting for your life and your sanity. And you're terrified. But you're still able to control your body enough to move around and function, at least for now.

What do you do?

The story continues ...

In total frustration, with tears streaming down my cheeks, I begged God to help me.

And the following day, I got a phone call.

My Salvation

<u>Sunday, October 3rd</u>

I woke up late again, thanking God that I finally got some sleep. I made breakfast for everyone while doing my best to ignore the insistent voice of Robert, who spoke to me in my head, telling me whatever he thought would get me to pay attention to him.

We needed to pick up some chicken feed that day, so I asked Nate's dad if he'd come along for the ride. We loaded everyone up into our four-door truck and headed out to the feed store.

On the way back, we decided to stop for ice cream at our favorite ice cream place, a farm out in the sticks that made their own ice cream with milk from their own cows. The kids chattered with each other, reading the flavors and trying to decide, while I stood back and focused on singing Disney tunes to myself to shut Robert up.

Once we got our food, we walked over to a picnic table to eat. There was a small petting zoo and playground they could play in, and they bounced in their seats, unable to decide whether the goats and bunnies were more exciting than the ice cream.

Just as I was sitting down to eat my own small cup of ice cream, my cell phone rang.

"Hello?"

"Hi, I'm calling for Amelia South," said the deep voice of an elderly but sturdy-sounding man.

"This is Amelia," I replied.

"Hi Amelia. I'm Bryan Redfield. Your dad asked me to call you and said I might be able to help you. What's wrong?"

I paused everything I was doing, stunned for a moment. Part of me had already decided that I'd just have to live with voices inside my head forever, so I was just going to eat my ice cream and survive this day. I had completely forgotten that my dad said he would ask someone to help me.

So, I told him everything.

"I'm possessed by a 17th century American soldier named Robert who was pretending to be a demon after he pretended to be a bunch of Native American spirits from this Sanctuary and medicine men graveyard I found and now he won't get out of my head or leave me alone even though a priest tried to exorcise him and we did a big drum ceremony yesterday that didn't work either." I took a breath, my heart racing.

Silence on the other end, but only for a moment. "Hi, Robert," Bryan said congenially.

"Hi," Robert responded cautiously with my voice.

"She just doesn't get it, does she?" Bryan said.

I could feel my lips curl into a slight smile. "Nope," Robert said.

"You know what I'm going to do for you, Robert?"

"What?"

"I'm going to make you stronger. Does that sound good to you?"

A bigger smile now. "Yes!"

"Good. Now, let me just take some notes…"

So, Robert and I both took turns pouring our hearts out to Bryan. Robert's story twisted and wound all over the place. My story revolved around everything that Robert had tricked me into believing. I told him that Robert had not let me sleep in days and I was barely able to eat or drink. I was running on fumes and didn't know how much longer I could last. Robert defended himself saying he just wanted my attention.

My attention was almost entirely on the conversation with Bryan. The kids finished their ice cream, and we piled into the truck again. Nate drove us up to one of our favorite hiking spots to show his dad, and I talked with Bryan the entire way, sitting in the back seat with my kids.

Robert spoke to Bryan with my mouth. His voice wasn't much deeper than mine, but he made crass jokes and references as a man would do and occasionally, he would blow a raspberry at the phone if he felt insulted. Robert told Bryan that he was my brother from a past life who had decided to inhabit my body to play a trick on me.

On the hiking trail, while I walked behind my kids and everyone else, Bryan told me, "I don't want to take your kids, I don't want any money, I don't want to have sex with you, I don't want to hurt you. There is nothing in this for me but good karma. Do you want my help?"

Without hesitation and not understanding what I was getting into, I replied "Yes!"

We had already been on the phone for over an hour, but both Robert and I were entranced by the deep, soothing voice on the other end of the line and didn't care how long we spoke.

"Okay then," he said, and I could hear his fingers tap-

 Uncovering *Amy*

ping on a keyboard in the background on his end. "Let me ask you this first, Robert. Do you think you can let Amelia get some sleep tonight?"

Robert hesitated. "Yes, I can do that," he said finally.

"Good. Thank you. Amelia?"

"Yeah?"

"I need to explain to you that Robert is not a demon. What has happened here is that the wall between your conscious mind and subconscious mind has been cut down and no longer exists. It's going to take us awhile, but your problem is fixable, okay?"

My brow furrowed, trying to comprehend what he meant. "So, like I can see and talk to dead people because I have a direct line to my subconscious?"

Bryan let out a breath. "Maybe you can, maybe you can't. That's up to Robert to decide. Right Robert?"

"Yeah," Robert replied, though his tone sounded like he didn't really understand either.

"I have to let you go now," Bryan said after we'd been talking for over two hours. At this point I had been walking hand in hand with my daughter down the easy paved part of the trail while the others waited behind.

"No!" Robert cried, gripping the cell phone. "I don't want you to!"

"It's okay, Robert," Bryan said soothingly. "I promise I will call you tomorrow and talk with you again. There's a book I need you to get a copy of that will help you through this and some other things we need to talk about before we get started. Are you feeling better now?"

Robert pouted for a moment. "Yes," he said eventually. "I'll let her sleep too."

"Thank you, Robert. I'm sure she appreciates that. And Amelia?"

"Yes?"

"Robert is your friend. He has known you far longer than you realize. He's going to be your best friend. He's there to protect you and love you. Right Robert?"

"Right!" Robert said, though I didn't really believe him.

"Okay, I have to get going now. I'll call you tomorrow when I'm awake. I'm in Arizona so I'm three hours behind you."

"Okay," I replied. "Thank you so much! I really appreciate this."

"You're very welcome. Bye now."

And he hung up. The sun was beginning to set, and dinner time was fast approaching. I needed to get everyone back home.

Lana looked up at me and said, "Are you okay now Mommy?"

I looked at her and gave her a big hug. "I'm okay now honey. I love you very, very much. Thank you for helping me."

She smiled. "You're welcome!" And we walked back to the main path to rejoin Nate and the others.

A Complete Reset

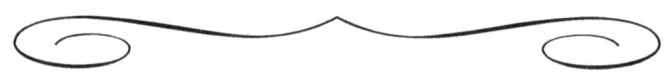

The next day I woke up a bit later than usual and simply lay in bed relaxing for a few extra minutes, delighted that I'd finally gotten a whole night of sleep.

I'm still here, Robert told me in my head. Is that okay?

I shrugged. "There's not anything I can do about it. We might as well try to be friends," I replied.

"What's that?" Nate asked. My voice had startled him awake.

"Sorry honey," I said apologetically. "It's time to get up."

Later that afternoon, Bryan called me. I could feel my tension ease the moment I heard his voice. It was as if part of me was gripping onto him for dear life—the one other person who actually seemed to understand what was going on inside me and was able to offer real help.

I could barely get a word in edgewise at first. Robert

wouldn't stop talking, spinning an even wilder tale to Bryan than he had yesterday. Eventually, Bryan had enough and asked Robert to let me talk with him.

"I need you to start journaling," he said. "It's going to help you a lot to get all your feelings and experiences written down on paper. That way it will be easier for you to see the progress you make over time. Do you have a pen and paper?"

I jumped up and grabbed an empty art journal I'd started sketching in recently. "Yes, go ahead."

I want you to write this down now and make a copy to hang up on the wall. Put it somewhere you'll be able to see it and read it every day. This is incredibly important, you understand?"

I nodded solemnly, even though I knew he couldn't see me over the phone. "I understand. Go ahead."

"I like, love, trust, accept, respect, and protect myself and Robert totally, completely, and unconditionally at all times, under any and all circumstances and conditions. Read it back to me."

I read it back and he said "Good. You need to look at that every day. Whether you know it or not, Robert and you are going to become closer. It will be the closest relationship you've ever experienced in your life."

"Really?" I asked incredulously. "How can that happen if he's inside my head?"

"That doesn't matter right now," Bryan replied. "All that matters is you know that he's there for you.

"When do you go to the bathroom?"

"What?!"

"When do you go to the bathroom?" he repeated. After a couple seconds of me trying to think of a response, he answered himself: "Whenever you need to. That's how often you will write in your journal."

"Ohhhh," I said, finally getting it. "What am I supposed to do about Robert pretending he can talk to other dead Native Americans? He might not be a demon, but I don't want another ghost inhabiting my body. What do I do if he tried to drive my body off a cliff or something? And what do I do when he lies to me again?"

Bryan sighed. "Robert does not want to hurt you. Write that down. Stop putting labels on everything. Also, you need to stop being judgmental. You're looking at all of this through eyes that have no idea what's actually going on. Right now, you don't know how to deal with Robert in a way that is positive, healthy, or constructive for both of you.

"Stop beating yourself up for the decisions you made and the mistakes you made that led you up to this point. It's okay to make mistakes! This is a learning process. When you beat yourself up for every little thing, you're fighting a battle you cannot win. Stop passing judgment on what's going on. You gain nothing from that. Judge the results, not the process. Do you understand what I mean?"

"I think so…"

"Right now, you are gathering research. You're watching what happens and trying to get along with him. Write this down: Robert is here to help me. I want you do two things that will help you out and get this process started."

"Okay, what?" I poised my pen above the page again.

"First, I want you to buy the book I'm OK You're OK[11]. You need to read that book before we can really get started resolving the damage that led to Robert coming out the way he did. Next, I want you to get a pillow that you can hug or sleep with. That pillow is Robert. I want you to sleep with him and hug him every night when you go to bed."

My eyebrows lifted. "Isn't that going to be weird?"

Bryan sighed again. "That's a judgment call. It's only weird if you think it's weird."

"Alright, I'll see what I can do. And I'll get that book on eBay right away."

"Good," he replied.

"Bryan?" Robert asked.

"Yes?"

"Can we talk again tomorrow?"

I could hear the smile in Bryan's voice. "Of course we can," he said kindly. Then we ended the conversation.

I ordered the book right away, but of course there was a delay with shipping. Over the next two weeks, I was desperate for the book to come in so we could get started. I still had to go about my life, working on the farm and with my mother, taking care of Nate and the kids, canning and preserving my harvest.

Every day, Bryan called me in the early afternoon to talk. I stopped wanting to talk to anyone else—after all, the other spiritual experts and friends I knew had been unable to help me in my desperate time of need. No one seemed to "get it" like Bryan did.

He told me I was going through "Spiritual Puberty." This whole thing was some kind of test from either God or my Higher Self.

"Don't put labels on things," he reminded me over and over, especially when I asked him if he and I could be friends. "Take notes, just watch what happens. You'll be wrong until it's over."

I loved talking with him, partly because it fed my need for acceptance and partly because it kept Robert calm. I admit I even flirted with Bryan over the phone, which I would have been terrified to do in person. He told me he was 70 years old but that he took good care of himself, exercising every day and following a strict diet. I found companionship in him for that, as I had eliminated many harmful foods from my own diet and was trying to do better to eat more wild foraged foods and mostly vegetables that I grew myself.

"Let go of control, in pieces," he told me one day. "Take back control when you feel you need to in order to understand what's going on. It's okay to be scared. It's okay to face the unknown. The solution is to have faith. The Universe is either taking care of me, or it isn't."

"Seeing as I was about to be committed to a mental institution when suddenly you got dropped in my lap, I'd say I'm being taken care of," I replied.

"I would say so," he agreed. "You need to be willing to face the unknown and give up control."

"But it's hard. I'm afraid to let go of control over my life. You don't understand, I have always had everything planned far ahead. I'm a farmer."

"It's only hard because you make it hard," he said. "Now write this down: The person I am becoming I have always been."

I wrote it. "I like that," I said with a smile.

"What you're going through right now is normal. The

steps are the same for everyone, all that's different are the details. Your spiritual side is knocking down the wall between your conscious and your subconscious mind. Everything you do in life is controlled by your subconscious mind. Everything you know you have learned because of your five senses: taste, touch, sight, smell, hearing. What you're experiencing now are senses that you cannot see. What sense tells you something is wrong when you get a 'gut feeling?' You can't explain it, but it happens anyway."

"You know, you're right!" I said in disbelief.

"Of course. You will continue to feel frazzled if you keep trying to use your five senses to understand what's going on right now. You spent your whole life depending on your five senses but now it's time to develop those other senses, the ones you can't see."

"I'm having so much trouble letting go of control though. I'm afraid Robert will hurt me."

"When you let go of control, you actually gain more control because you're no longer limited to the things you can control. Insecure people won't let go of control because they don't trust the Universe or God. If God is taking care of you, you have nothing to fear."

"I'm not Christian, you know."

"You don't have to be Christian or religious. My own belief system was thrown out the window when I died after a car accident I had when I was 10. They brought me back to life, but I always knew there was more to life than what the Church taught after that. I still believe in a higher power, and it's easier to call it God than anything else."

"Wow," I said. "Yeah, I guess you're right."

I didn't understand it yet, but I was going to.

The book finally arrived in my mailbox, nearly two weeks after I started talking with Bryan. I was so excited, that I ran up to my bedroom and sat on the bed to start reading it while I was home alone.

The preface was mildly interesting, but the first chapter stopped me in my tracks. "Throughout history one impression of human nature has been consistent: that man has a multiple nature." (Harris, 1967, p. 21)

I could feel Robert freeze. He didn't want me to read the book.

Stop. No! I'm going to call the other spirits to come and make you stop, he said insistently in my head. He even tried to stop me from lifting the book to my eyes.

"Cut that out!" I told him. I pulled the book up and kept reading.

"When Sigmund Freud appeared on the scene in

the early twentieth century, the enigma was sub-
jected to a new probe, the discipline of scientific
inquiry. Freud's fundamental contribution was
his theory that the warring factions existed in the
unconscious. Tentative names were given to the
combatants: the Superego became thought of as
the restrictive, controlling force over the Id (in-
stinctual drives), with the Ego as a referee operat-
ing out of "enlightened self-interest." (Harris,
1967, p. 22)

"Holy shit," I said to myself, setting the book down in
my lap.

Up until this point, I was still under the impression
(trusting fool that I was) that Robert was a 17th century
soldier who had somehow jumped into my head near
the Sanctuary and that I was going to be forced to live
with this possession forever because there was no real
way to exorcise it out.

I could feel Robert whining and crying inside my head.
The jig was up.

"You're part of me. Holy crap, how could I be so stupid?
You're part of my subconscious mind!"

Robert blew a raspberry at me and pouted in the corner
inside my head. I finally understood.

I called Bryan.

"I got the book and I started reading it and he didn't

want me to, but I kept reading it anyway. He's part of me," I said excitedly after our greetings were exchanged. "Robert is part of me!"

Bryan huffed a proud little breath. "Good for you," he said, but it was in a proud father sort-of-way, not condescending. "It's about time you figured that out. Now we just need to know which part. Keep reading the book."

"What are you going to do with him?" I asked.

"We're going to reprogram him to make him stronger. And the two of you are going to get closer. I promise."

Bryan and Robert talked for a few minutes. Bryan helped him understand that it was necessary for Amelia to learn the truth in order for us to grow together. Eventually I started asking Bryan more questions.

"The more scared you are, the more courage you have when you face that fear," Bryan told Robert lovingly. "You need to forgive yourself for the mistakes you made and make amends with Amelia." Robert huffed in response but begrudgingly agreed that Bryan was right.

I was in awe of the way he was able to handle Robert. "Where did you learn all this stuff?"

"Well I went to school for psychology," he explained. "I got my AA in Psychology in San Bernardino, California, then I went on to study more at UCLA. Unfortunately, I ran out of money for college about 15 credits away from graduation, so I had to stop there. But I also read many books, including Psycho Cybernetics[12], The Primal Scream[13], and many others, as well as studying with some of the top hypnotherapists in the area at the time."

"So, they taught you how to heal schizophrenia?"

"Haha! No, I had my own journey to follow. I taught myself, using the tools I was given by several mentors as well as what I like to call the School of Hard Knocks. I've been doing this for myself and others, and getting better and better each time, for over 40 years now. And by the way, you're not schizophrenic."

"Are you sure?" I asked dubiously.

"Positive. Because neither am I. And I went through almost the exact same thing you're going through now. It's just the details were different."

"Wow," I said again.

I was absolutely star-struck at this point. I had never heard anyone talk about this sort of thing. Lots of people lauded mental health drugs, therapy, and even meditation techniques. But no one I had ever heard of told you how to understand what was really going on.

I read I'm OK You're OK. It changed my understanding of everything that was going on in my mind. When I'd finally finished two weeks later, after our daily chats Bryan and I had decided that we were friends now.

"The book does a fantastic job of explaining the three main parts of your personality: Parent, Adult, and Child," he explained. "But it doesn't tell you anything about how to resolve their problems or teach them how to work together. That's what I had to figure out on my own."

The most important thing we discovered in the time it took me to read the book was that Robert wasn't really Robert.

One day Bryan finally told me that he had figured out who Robert was.

"Robert is a little boy," he said carefully.

"Really?!" I exclaimed, genuinely surprised.

"Yes," Bryan said. "He's your inner child."

"Huh. Shouldn't my inner child be a girl?" I asked. I thought for a minute. "I mean, I've been a tomboy most of my life. I guess it's no surprise that he's a boy."

"Ppppllllllbbbbppllllllltht!" Robert blew a raspberry at me into the phone.

"Sorry about that," I said to Bryan.

"What's the matter Robert?" Bryan asked.

"None of your business!" Robert said indignantly.

It only took a few more days to figure out the problem. Robert was my inner child, yes. But he wasn't a little boy.

Bryan had taught me how to communicate with Robert and "see" him inside my mind, and in my dreams. One day I was lying in bed with my eyes closed, trying to communicate with and see him. I saw this little kid, maybe 3 or 4 years old, with ratty hair cut short, run past me. I hadn't seen the front of the kid, just a naked butt from behind. I figured it must be Robert.

But the next time I saw him, just as I was falling asleep, the face had changed and the child was wearing a nightgown. The hair had grown a little longer and the face was shy and coy.

Robert was a little girl.

She had pretended to be a boy to protect herself. Just as I had pretended to be a boy (or a tomboy) for years in my childhood.

I approached her gently (in my mind's eye), crouched down, and said, "Hi! What's your name?"

She came up onto my lap, wrapped her arms around my neck, and said "Amy."

That night, I brought the pillow I had bought to bed with me and hugged it tightly. "I love you, Amy," I said, feeling a bit silly.

But Amy hugged right back. I could feel her smile and calm down.

All she ever wanted was to be loved and accepted. And now, she was finally going to get that.

The Super Team

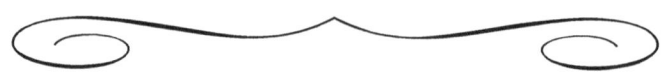

Bryan developed a method for removing negative beliefs and habits from your personality and reprogramming your subconscious mind with positive beliefs. He took me through many sessions, starting with Amy.

It's a bit like being hypnotized: you lay down someplace quiet and comfortable, close your eyes, and go into an inner room in your mind that he helps you create. As long as you're capable of visualizing things inside your mind, the method works. He brought Amy out several times to remove her negative programming and replace it with positive programming, non-judgmental and humble.

I would get up on the platform inside my head to have the negativity removed and while inside my mind it was as simple as watching a little girl be magically cleansed of her dark thoughts, in the real world, my head shook violently from side to side as if saying No! over and over again. I told Bryan that this had been happening and what he said stuck with me ever since.

Uncovering *Amy*

"That's your negative programming fighting for its life. It doesn't want to leave. It's afraid of the unknown. All it's known is the fears and habits you've had up 'til now. Don't worry, the positive programming will stick, and you'll feel better soon." Then we continued the session.

One day, Bryan called while I was out taking a walk on a nature trail. I answered happily as he greeted both me and Amy. Then he asked a question I wasn't expecting.

"Who would like to come out next?"

It was a simple, straightforward question. I realized in that moment that there was another personality (we called them "entities" after this point) who was ready to let herself be known.

"My sexual side," I answered. I was beginning to get the hang of "letting go of control," as Bryan says. What it really meant for me was that I needed to allow my conscious mind, the original Amelia, to step aside and let whoever needed to speak to him speak.

"Well, hi there," he said congenially.

"Fuck you!" she spat, through my mouth.

"Oh, is that your name?" he asked sarcastically.

"No, it's Alaina," she replied. "But you can go fuck yourself."

"Okay then, you don't want to talk with me," he said simply. And he addressed me. "So, how's your day going Amelia?"

"Wait!" Alaina cried. "No, I do want to talk. I need help," she explained.

"I don't want to fight you, Alaina. What can I do for you?"

By the end of our conversation, Alaina had let out all the sexual frustrations I'd had over my entire life from puberty through now. I had a long history of being the "giver" in a relationship and allowing the men to get their rocks off without expecting my needs to be met in return.

He explained the three types of sex (Fucking, Recreational Sex, and Making Love) and informed me without any minced words that I had only ever experienced Fucking before.

I had a lot of pent-up sexual frustration. And I'd experienced a lot of emotional and mental abuse, both from my sexual partners and the father figures in my life.

It all got resolved inside the inner room.

After Alaina came my Inner Parent, Mary. Then my Feminine side, Selena. Each time a new part of my personality decided they were brave enough to emerge, Bryan praised them for having the courage to come out and took the time needed to remove their negative programming and replace it with positive programming.

He told me to think of my inner self (my mind) like a glass. It's as if shortly after I was born someone picked up the glass and dropped it on the floor. The glass shattered—some large pieces, and many small pieces and fragments. The larger pieces ended up receiving more abuse from the outside world and becoming larger pieces of my personality. The smaller pieces and fragments had been able to hide in the deep recesses of my mind, but receiving negative programming, nonetheless. Each one of them had an influence on my outward behaviors, habits, and overall personality.

You see, from the moment of conception through around 6 years old, a person receives most (if not all) of the mental programming that will make them who they are in the future. Say for example that 2-year-old you watches over and over when your dad comes home from work and screams at your mom to have dinner hot and ready on the table for him, becoming verbally or physically abusive to her if his demands are not met. Or say you're three and you walk into the bathroom to find your mom staring at herself in the mirror, fretting over the fat that's collecting on her thighs or the hair above her lip.

In the first scenario, your father has taught you that this is the way to treat a woman. If you're a little boy, you will grow up to be an abusive partner, belittling your girlfriend or wife any time she doesn't do things exactly the way you think she should. If you're a little girl, you learn that this is the appropriate way for you to be treated by any man you date or marry, and you will suffer the abuse knowing that it's perfectly normal and you're meant to be treated that way.

In the second scenario, if you're a girl you learn that you're not ever supposed to be pleased with your physical appearance. There's always something to pick apart, something not perfect about you no matter what you do. You're never happy with the way you look. If you're a boy, this might also affect you in the same way or you may have unrealistic beauty standards for any woman you date in your future. She's too hairy, or too fat, or her hair isn't the right shade, etc. You carry the same prejudices that your parents (or whoever raised you) instill in you at a young age throughout the rest of your life, no matter who your future partner may be.

Every one of the pieces of your mental glass, from the biggest chunk (your dominant personality, most often your inner Parent) to the tiniest fleck of glass dust, are part of the whole. When you're shattered, the pieces develop separately from one another and have a tendency to argue or fight with each other until one or a few of them win out and take control of your personality.

But when you can remove these negative thought patterns and reprogram your subconscious beliefs, the pieces are slowly put back together again. Eventually, they all begin to work together harmoniously. This is your Super Team™.

Uncovering *Amy*

Bryan calls this Super Team™ training. Each ST training session follows the same basic format, but the positive programming is tweaked each time to reflect the needs of whichever team member is being reprogrammed.

For example, I recall one session where he was reprogramming the part of me responsible for getting angry or upset at bad drivers on the road. During the reprogramming phase of the training, one of the things he said was "You always remain calm when you're driving, regardless of what the other people on the road are doing. You focus on driving safely and getting to your destination without incident. You never allow your anger at another person's bad driving to impede your own ability to drive safely."

Yes, to the naked eye, this sounds like a simple affirmation. But when added as part of the overall training session, these positive behaviors are imprinted in the mind and eventually become a permanent part of your personality.

It's been nearly four years since I started Super Team Training with Bryan and while I stabilized into my new self within the first 6-12 months, I still occasionally have fragmented parts of my personality show up and ask to be reprogrammed. And thankfully, I now know what to do on my own if I need to.

Some Serious Changes

After Alaina came out and got reprogrammed, the two most abused parts of me (my inner child and my sexual side) were now at peace and working together.

With the target cards Bryan gave me, I was getting better at allowing myself to let go of control, I had ceased apologizing for every little thing I did whether it was my fault or not, and I had finally started to truly like, love, trust, accept, respect, and protect myself and my Super Team under all circumstances and conditions.

This is the foundation of the training.

But it's not everything. Bryan also played the role of therapist to me. The way he explained it was that once you get your mental health back, it's easier to see dysfunction in other people. For him, spotting the dysfunctional parts of my personality was easy. And he had the experience to be able to talk me through a lot of the changes that had begun to happen in my life.

First, we finally figured out what had happened to me in the beginning. Yes, I had been introduced to the Sanctuary graveyard. But Amy had been so beaten up and upset for so long that she used the excuse of me talking with Indian Spirits as a way for her to come out and be seen. She was truly the bravest of all my inner entities because instead of continuing to hide inside me and continue being beaten down, she chose to come out and get my attention, one way or another. But her dysfunctional programming made her hide who she really was and pretend to be what she thought I wanted: a handsome man to love me.

This came from my abused sexual side; I spent my entire life thinking I was unattractive, not good enough, unpopular, unliked by guys (I was straight,) and knowing full well that my only worth as a woman was because I had big boobs and was able to get fucked and have babies. Amy thought if she pretended to be an attractive, strong man giving me the kind of attention I desperately craved in the real world that I would listen to her and give her the attention she desperately craved right back.

When I asked for help, the only people I knew to ask were the spiritualists, drummers, reiki practitioners, and astrologers whom I had been hanging around for the last year or more. Every step of the way, my delusions had been fed and supported by these people, until it all came to a head when Amy decided to stop pretending. That was when I realized that none of those people who I had loved, respected, trusted, and looked up to for their guidance had any clue what was really going on inside me, what was wrong, how to actually help me.

Please understand: these are not bad people. They're good people with good intentions. But when they did what they knew how to do and it didn't work, rather than try to understand it and help me, they tipped their hats and said, "See ya" and walked away.

They walked away because I didn't fit into their belief system. I was proof their belief system was wrong, but they couldn't deal with that so the easiest thing for them to do was to just block it out and walk away. And that's what they did.

I found this process of blocking things out and just walking away is very common in Life in all fields, especially religion, with insecure people. People who are secure are open to these kinds of things because they want to learn about Life rather than trying to control Life and make it adjust to their beliefs.

For insecure people it's a losing battle. Some learn that voluntarily. Some are forced to learn it. Some never learn it and take their faulty belief system with them to the grave.

Bryan picked up the pieces. He was the only one who saw what was actually going on and knew how to help me.

What ended up happening over the months of being reprogrammed by him, is that I regained my self-respect and my mental health for the first time in my entire life.

I gained it piece by piece, one day at a time. Bryan always went at my pace. He knew I could only learn and absorb this so fast. So, he adjusted everything to my pace.

Because of Bryan's experience and expertise as a dating coach, he taught me how a romantic relationship could be a partnership, rather than a one-sided fight where one person is the clear winner and the other person is the clear loser. He said, "When you have a clear winner and loser then you have an abusive relationship. It's a Givers/Takers relationship. Givers always end up with Takers and Takers always end up with Givers. It's a great arrangement for the Taker but a really bad arrangement for the Giver. The Taker always wins because he keeps the Giver in place by saying, 'You're being selfish.' The Giver feels guilty and continues to let the Taker abuse them. When the Giver finally gets fed up and leaves, they get involved with, you guessed it, another Taker because that's what they're programmed to believe is all they're worth."

And he taught me about the third option, which was incredibly rare: Sharers. This is when two people try equally hard to make each other happy mentally, emotionally, spiritually, physically and sexually.

It's a true Partnership with no games, tricks, manipulation or abuse by either one of them.

Sharers refuse to put up with, tolerate or waste their time with a Taker. Sharers know really fast when they're dealing with a Taker. They don't get mad. They don't try to get even. Once they realize they're dealing with a Taker then Sharers just pick themselves up, dust themselves off and walk away. That's one of the huge benefits of gaining true mental health.

Once he taught me how to become a Sharer, and how to spot another Sharer, my whole life changed for the better. He said that becoming a Sharer is part of gaining true mental health.

Once he taught me the truth about what a romantic relationship is meant to be like, I could see that my marriage to Nate was a sham. I had been acting as his Mother and he was basically a good little boy doing whatever I told him to do.

I decided that was not what I wanted in my life anymore and we got divorced.

The next big realization came when I had a friend and her kids over for dinner. I hadn't seen her for the last month. This woman had been one of my oldest and closest friends for the longest time, but for the first time in my life I could see that she was terribly negative, fearful, and ungrateful. I found myself drinking more wine than I should just to stand being around her and her husband and praying for them to leave early.

The next day, with a clear head, I finally realized, understood and accepted that the reason we had been so close is because that's how negative I used to be. Now that I wasn't negative anymore, I couldn't stand being around her. I'd completely outgrown the level she was on, and I couldn't take it anymore. I also realized, understood and accepted there was absolutely nothing I could do to help her so I did the only thing I could: I walked away completely. I never hung out with them again after that.

I also eventually realized, understood and accepted you don't outgrow people. Rather, you outgrow the spiritual and emotional level they're on. And once you've outgrown it then you never go back. Yes, that hurts, but it hurt because I was passing judgment on it rather than accepting it as a normal part of growth.

Little by little, as I gained more respect for myself and confidence in my skills and abilities, the people who did not match the new me slowly slipped away.

I got a new job working as a manager on a farm. I met new people and proved to myself that I was a damn good farmer when I had the resources to put into it.

I eventually stopped talking to my sister completely, after realizing that I did not deserve to suffer her abuse and wouldn't stand for it any longer.

I stopped communicating with my mother, who had taught me that my breasts were what I needed to get a good husband and that money could solve all your problems.

I stopped talking with my father, who had always wanted a boy and had been disappointed that I was a girl. He taught me that a man who screams verbal abuse at, and does not respect or love his wife, is a perfectly good, normal husband.

Bryan told me it's very common for people who gain true mental health to end their relationships with some or all of their family. He told me not to get upset over it.

He said, "Just because you're no longer dysfunctional doesn't mean they are or that they're ready to change."

It ended up costing my sister, my mother and my father their relationship with me. And I couldn't be happier.

He told me, "You have to 'live and let live' and be non-judgmental. Just walk away with no explanation because no matter what you said they wouldn't understand. They'd blame you. It isn't worth it."

I became so comfortable with who I was that I stopped drinking alcohol completely. I didn't need it anymore. Why would I need to drink and hurt my physical body when the whole reason to drink was so I could let Amy or Alaina come out and be themselves for a while? I didn't have to "let" these parts of me come out because they were out all the time. We simply coexisted all at the same time, happily together.

Whoever was best suited for a specific job would come out and be the dominant personality while she was needed.

For example: My inner Adult was the best one to teach people about herbalism or doing all the homestead work. If it was time to play with my kids, Amy would gleefully run and skip and play with them.

Sometimes it's a combination of who's best suited to handling a situation. Then it's a matter of two heads (or more) are better than one.

Finally, everyone inside my head was working as one cohesive whole as I grew and evolved into a confident, whole woman. It's just like a baby: it grows and slowly but surely, through trial and error, learns how to use its physical body. Gaining your mental health works the same way.

Bryan always says, "The person you are becoming you have always been." That is the theme of Super Team™ training. Bringing out the Complete Woman (or person) you have always had hidden deep inside you.

Eventually, in early 2023, after several months of being unable to find another farm job, I threw myself into running my small farm business full-time. I'd had a love for foraging wild foods and medicinal plants for many years and had just started leading some workshops and foraging walks and I figured I'd give a shot at making a real living doing it.

There have been ups and downs, and many various facets to my business. Today I teach foraging walks, I built an entire library of online herbalism and foraging classes, I make and sell herbal healing products, I create content for social media, and I do personal health consultations. And I LOVE doing it.

Not one of my customers, followers, or anyone who meets me has any idea that I have an entire team of women (well, there's one guy, my masculine side, but he's way outnumbered) running the show inside my head. I have grown confident in myself, my physical appearance, my skills and abilities, and my business. I'm at peace. And it's all because of Super Team™ training.

It's all because when I was at my wits' end, begging for help in my darkest hour, the Universe handed me the one man who could help me on a silver platter.

No one gets mental health by accident. It's a long, lonely and often painful road. But once you truly have it then you'll know what every mentally healthy person knows by heart: Whatever it costs it's more than worth it.

BRYAN REDFIELD

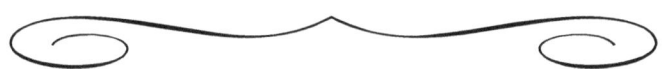

How can I prove I'm not crazy to people who are? We read the world wrong and then we say that it deceives us.

> "Damn it, Boss. I like you too much not to say it. You've got everything, except one thing, madness. A man needs a little madness or else he never dares cut the rope and be free."
>
> Zorba, from the movie, *Zorba the Greek*, starring Anthony Quinn.

That Zorba quote is a cornerstone of how I've lived my life. It's given me the strength to cut the rope and be free, allowed me the freedom to be myself, and has helped me to see Life for what it is rather than what I want it to be.

"Ye shall know the truth and the truth shall make you free." John 8:32

The second quote helps keep me on track when I completely misinterpret a person, relationship, job or anything else.

People ask me how I came up with the Super Team™ training.

I created it for myself. I didn't create it for anyone else.

I created it one painful day at a time. I was miserable and had no self-confidence. I didn't like myself or my job. I also kept getting involved in abusive relationships. I was a Giver who kept getting involved with Takers. And I didn't know why or how to stop it. I kept beating myself up and I couldn't stop. I couldn't figure out what was wrong or how to fix it. The therapists I went to were basically glorified babysitters who sat there and listened … but offered no help. I got better results from talking with the drunks in the bar than I did with them.

But I'm getting ahead of myself.

Let's start at the beginning.

I was born Christopher Brian Redfield on December 20, 1950 in Rockville Center, Long Island, New York, USA.

I have two brothers. One is a year and a half older and one is five and a half years younger.

My parents got divorced when I was 7. My Dad was an alcoholic. My Mom finally got fed up and accepted he wasn't going to stop drinking so she left and divorced him. She got full custody of my brothers and me.

We moved from New York to Marlboro, Massachusetts. It was as far away from my dad as she could get. She chose Marlboro because her sister, my aunt, lived there. We lived in the house right next to theirs. My uncle, her husband, was a high school teacher, a bully, and a real pain in the ass. He would bully my brothers and me frequently because he knew we couldn't fight back. He was very unfair, but the details don't matter and aren't necessary. We lived there for several years.

Eventually mom got remarried to a wonderful man. He was a great stepfather. He helped raise the three of us and was a great role model. I love him and respect him very much.

Eventually we moved back to New York because that's where my stepfather's job was.

We landed in Dobbs Ferry, New York. My brothers and I went through the Dobbs Ferry Public School system, from which I graduated in 1969. I was ranked number 69 in a class of 102 graduates.

Dad and I were very close, my dad lived on Long Island, New York. On the weekends when I was in my teens, I'd sometimes get on a train in Dobbs Ferry to go see my dad. It took me to Grand Central Station in New York, where Dad would meet me.

He didn't have much money, so he lived in a furnished

room. We would sit in his room and play penny ante poker for hours and talk father to son—I cherish those times.

When I got home to Dobbs Ferry my mother would take her hatred and resentment towards my father out on me. It wasn't a fun time.

I wasn't looking for trouble and I wasn't a troublemaker. I was a good kid who was victimized in the truest sense because there wasn't anything I could do about it. This went on for years.

Mom had a standard line when we fought: "If you don't like the way we do things here you can pack your bags and go." This was the 1960s. There was no place for me to go and I knew it. That fact got crammed down my throat for years and there was nothing I could do about it except bide my time.

One time when I was 17 years old, I came back from spending a weekend with Dad. Mom got really mad and said her standard line during a fight, "If you don't like the way we do things here you can pack your bags and go."

I looked her straight in the eye and said with total honesty and no hostility, "Mom, pretty soon I'm going to turn 18. Then I'm going to graduate from high school. Then I'm going to move out, and you'll never see me again."

The look on my mom's face was total shock. I'd never fought back before because I couldn't. There's something about a 17-year-old young man telling you that with total sincerity that is completely disarming. There is no defense against it. She never said that to me again because she knew I meant it.

The day after I graduated from high school, I left New York because I had a job in Nantucket, Massachusetts as a cook in a restaurant. I'd worked there when I was a junior in high school during summer the year before and they loved me. They offered me a job the following year when I was a senior and I gladly took it.

When summer ended, I moved in with Dad on Long Island, New York. He'd remarried and was living in an apartment with his wife. I was 19 years old and as innocent and naïve as they come: I had zero street smarts and no job skills. What kind of job skills can a 19-year-old man have?

I got a job working at the Post Office as a mailman. I have nothing but respect for the Post Office and all of its employees. I don't mean to sound unkind but being a mailman isn't that hard. It wasn't a job for the old because back then you had so much walking to do. But for me at 19 it was great exercise. Now they drive using a Postal Vehicle or their own vehicle and get compensated for gas. But back then it required a lot of walking.

My point is that I was quick to see that just having a high school education meant I wasn't going to be getting any kind of job that would make me a lot of money, so I started looking at colleges to go to.

Back then, before computers and the internet, the only way to look at the colleges was at the public library. So that's where I went. I had a low grade point average in high school because I was so unhappy; I just did the bare minimum to get by.

I never considered myself to be very smart. After my mother told me I was stupid and worthless for so many years, I believed it. My self-confidence was non-existent.

When I was a senior one high school guidance counselor was smart enough and cared enough to get me an IQ test. It turned out I had an IQ of 140. Not a genius but not stupid either. It changed my attitude toward myself.

Anyway, from doing my research in the library I found out some of the junior colleges in California had only two requirements: 1) you had to be 18 or older and 2) you had to speak English. I met both those qualifications, so I applied to a few of them.

Much to my shock and surprise, three of them accepted me!

I decided to go to San Bernardino Valley Junior College in San Bernardino, CA. My major was psychology and sociology.

I moved lock, stock, and barrel to San Bernardino. Anything I couldn't carry in one suitcase I threw away. I wanted to get as far away from New York and my family as possible, and California fit the bill perfectly.

I wanted to walk away from everything I had known and start my life again. This is one of the many times in my life that the Zorba quote at the beginning of this chapter helped me so much. It was 1970 and I was 19 years old.

When I moved to San Bernardino it was like I landed on a different planet. Their culture was completely different from life in New York and I loved it. They knew nothing about me and that's the way I wanted it.

I took to junior college like a duck takes to water. I loved it and the fact that I didn't have to put up with anyone in my family. Back then when you made a call you had to pay by the minute so that was my number one reason for not calling anyone. It eliminated my calling anyone.

One day it sank in on me that if I got run over by a car no one would know who I was or even care. It was a sobering thought and a necessary part of growing up. We all face that realization at some point in our lives, some earlier, some later. As scared as I was it all sank in, and I loved the freedom of being able to find out who I was, what I was and what I wanted out of life.

Psychology and sociology made so much sense to me. I understood it completely and my grades went from the Cs and Ds of high school to As and Bs. I loved it and after two years, I graduated with a 3.5 GPA. I transferred to UCLA. I continued to major in psychology and sociology and I loved it.

But UCLA was a shock. In junior college my classes were around 20 to 30 students per class. The teachers cared about you, and you could ask them questions. My smallest class at UCLA was 120. My cultural anthropology class was around 250 students, and my psychology class was around 350 students. To put that in perspective, my high school graduating class in 1969 had 102 graduates.

The teachers at UCLA couldn't have cared less about you. Grades were all done on a bell curve.

I remember one time in my psychology class at UCLA I raised my hand and asked the professor a question. He made a big joke out of my question and all the ass-kissing students laughed appropriately.

I raised my hand again. He said, "Yeah?" I very calmly said, "I don't mind your laughing at me, but I would like an answer to my question." There was dead silence in the class. He looked away and said, "I don't know the answer. That was a good question."

After that none of the students would sit near me. It was nice. I could sit down and there would be empty seats on my left, right, behind and in front of me. The next time I asked a question the professor said, "Yes, sir?" and he meant it.

At the end of my junior year, I ran out of money and had to get a job. Back in 1974 there weren't many jobs available. I took a job as a parking attendant in an apartment Highrise on Wilshire Boulevard in Los Angeles. I got paid minimum wage, but it gave me some time to think things out.

I wanted to get completely away from my mom and everyone in my family. I'd been beaten up and abused enough to last me the rest of my life. But I didn't know how to "cut the rope and be free."

I met a guy who was an extra in movies. He told me I should become an actor. I told him I didn't know anything about acting. He said, "Neither do I but I make a living at it."

So, I decided to study acting.

He said, "You should stop using your first name. Use your middle name and changed the 'i' to a 'y' because it will look better in print."

I realized that he gave me a way to sever all my ties to my past.

So, I stopped using my first name, Chris, and started going by my middle name with a "y".

Thus in 1974 Bryan Redfield was born and I completely killed Chris off.

Chris Redfield ceased to exist.

Over the next few years, I studied with three of the best acting teachers in Hollywood: Hope Summers, Nina Foch and Grant Williams. I learned the craft of acting from them and I loved it. I did several equity waver plays and worked with real professionals. I could talk with them and ask them questions. They all had answers I needed but couldn't get anywhere else.

I remember talking with a woman in one of my acting classes that was a student of the class just like me. We did a scene together. She asked me what I did for a job. I told her I was a parking attendant. She said, "Why don't you become a bartender? It's much better money and you leave every day with cash in your pocket from tips."

I did some research. The best bartending school at the time was run by a former bartender. He'd been a bartender for 30 years. I had very little money. I took my last $200 and paid for the course in full. I was desperate. The Zorba quote at the beginning of this chapter helped me a lot.

The course on how to become a bartender was a two-week course. I finished it in 8 days because I was desperate.

I was broke, and I needed a job. I looked in the newspapers. Back then that's how you got a job, by looking in the Classified Ads section of the newspaper. I was so desperate I just went from restaurant to restaurant, knocking on doors, not knowing if they needed a bartender or not, and tried to get a job. My biggest problem was I was just out of bartending school with no experience.

A week later I had my first bartender job. It was on the Sunset Strip in Hollywood. A week after that the manager was replaced in one of many nepotism events that happened in my life. I was on the receiving end. The new manager didn't care how good I was. He had "friends" who needed jobs, so I got fired after one week of work for no reason.

Welcome to the real world.

In 1977 I got a commercial agent. I took a course on how to get cast in commercials on TV and it helped me a lot. I started going on commercial acting interviews, where I learned a lot about the acting profession. I also learned the entertainment business, movies, TV, etc. doesn't run. It stumbles.

Later that year I made a national commercial for Gillette. It got me into the Screen Actors' Guild, the main union for actors. The commercial wasn't used but I didn't care. I was in the Screen Actors Guild. I was a legitimate actor.

I went through 11 bartending jobs in the first year. I could tell you stories you won't believe. It was Hollywood so I saw the best of the best and the worst of the worst. And it was all crammed down my throat.

I learned an important secret about getting a job: I'd write down on a piece of paper my ideal, perfect bartender job. Then with each new job, whether I got fired or quit, I'd write down two lists: What I liked about the job and what I didn't like. Then I'd revise my ideal job list. I'd add the things I liked and wrote out a list of the things I didn't want. This helped me a great deal.

The second year I was a bartender in Hollywood I only went through 7 jobs. I kept polishing my two lists after each job. If I didn't get fired and was able to quit when I wanted, then I polished my two lists on the job.

My third year as a bartender I only went through 2 jobs. I stayed at the last job for 11 years. So, I was a bartender in Hollywood for 14 years and I worked in 20 different bars and restaurants. I worked in everything from local bars and restaurants in Beverly Hills, to nightclubs and everything in between.

One job was at a strip joint in North Hollywood. I'd never been in a strip joint before, so I didn't know what to expect. When the owner hired me, he said, "You can't date the strippers." Oh yeah? Just watch.

After ONE DAY on the job, I knew it wasn't going to work. You gain your street smarts the only way that matters: The hard way by getting screwed over and learning from the experience so it doesn't happen again.

There was one stripper there who I was attracted to, and who was also attracted to me. I sat down at one of the chairs in front of an empty stage to gather my thoughts. She came and sat near me but not too close in case anyone was watching. I told her the truth. I said, "This job isn't going to work for me." She said, "I'm sorry you're quitting." I said, "Yeah. Do you want to stay in touch?" She smiled and said yes. She gave me her phone number. I asked her where she lived. I wasn't familiar with the town, so I asked her where it was. She said, "It's 40 miles away. I live with my father." What??? I told her I'd call her. I left and threw her phone number away. Why bother? That had "disaster" written all over it.

Afterward, I looked at my two lists again. I saw one of the items I'd written down was that I wanted to work in a place where I'd meet girls. Well, the strip joint HAD girls. I knew I had to revise that item on my list.

I had another bartender job that I'll tell you about. It was my first day on the job. I got my first drink order. It was for something simple, like a gin and tonic. I started to make the drink. The manager stood there and watched me. I didn't care. I was used to being watched.

As I made the drink he said, "You can't make that drink that way."

I innocently asked, "Why not?"

He said, "Because I don't like the way you're doing it."

I said, "Have you ever been a bartender?"

"No."

"Then how can you tell me how to make drinks?"

"I don't like the way you're doing it."

Then he proceeded to tell me how he wanted me to make the drink.

He was a joke. I looked him straight in the eye, held my hands up and said, "This isn't going to work out. Have a nice day." And I walked off the job.

The owner of the restaurant called me to ask me what happened. After I told him he apologized. I told him it was okay. Then I said, "That guy is going to put you out of business." He asked me if I wanted the manager job. I thanked him and told him I was a bartender, not a manager; we parted on good terms.

I got home and worked on my two lists and was able to figure out what I had left off and fixed it.

Hollywood gave me the best of the best and the worst of the worst. Often in one night.

While I was working as a bartender, I was taking acting classes and learning the craft. I was pursuing a career as an actor to the best of my ability … just like 200,000 other unemployed actors in Hollywood.

I play chess. I'm just an average player but I love the game.

I learned that the acting profession and becoming a successful actor are a lot like learning how to play chess: Imagine that you've never seen a chess game before. No one tells you the rules, who the power players are, how each piece moves, what their names are [King, Queen, Bishops, Knights, Castles and Pawns], how they move, the strengths and weaknesses of each piece, what the goal of the game is, how to win or what constitutes a win.

You'll know why that's so important later in this chapter.

I found being a good bartender is very similar to watching a chess game for the first time, too.

Here's a footnote I learned from a career bartender. He said, "Good bartenders know they have to remember some things and forget others. Great bartenders know what to remember and what to forget."

I never forgot that quote.

I would start every day that I worked as a bartender the same way. I punched in and was on the clock. Then just as I walked behind the bar I would say to myself, "Class is now in session."

One of the 20 different bars and restaurants I worked at during my 14 years as a bartender in Hollywood was Chippendales. It's a nightclub where guys dance on a stage to music and strip for women. It's adult entertainment for women. If you're not familiar with the place just Google Chippendales and you'll get a complete education.

It was around the time I worked at Chippendales that I

started having recurring bad dreams at night when I went to sleep. They started to upset me and, as much as I tried to ignore them, they kept coming back.

We've all had bad dreams, but recurring bad dreams? I was having this dream about once a week. Then twice a week. Then sometimes three times a week. Whatever was wrong, it was just getting worse.

I knew I had to deal with it. But how??? I didn't understand them and didn't know why it kept recurring. I didn't know how to handle the dreams, and I certainly didn't know what to do about them.

Unfortunately, I had no one to talk it out with who would understand what I was going through or how to help me.

During college, I studied Dream Analysis, so I had some idea of what was going on.

When these dreams started, I started to read books on the meaning of dreams, dream analysis and so on. I read every book I could get my hands on and learned a lot.

I learned I had to keep a dream journal. So, I wrote down every dream I had when I woke up in as much detail as I could remember. If I had a dream that was so upsetting that it woke me up in the middle of the night, then I wrote it down then and there. Then I went back to sleep.

They didn't know a lot about dreams back in the 1980s,

Uncovering *Amy*

but I was piecing it together myself one night at a time, one dream at a time. I had no one to talk it out with because, again, this was before the internet, and no one had a computer. So, I struggled with it alone.

Slowly but surely, I started to learn how to control my dreams. I was able to start talking with the people and creatures (for lack of a better word) in my dreams. Have you ever talked with a tree? How about a rock? How about talking with a car? It can get pretty crazy. And it did. I kept detailed notes in my journal.

One recurring dream I had was between the cartoon character "Popeye, The Sailor Man" (the guy who ate spinach to gain strength) and a small elf. Popeye would beat the shit out of this poor helpless elf. The dreams got progressively worse until I started writing them down. The dreams made absolutely no sense to me. Why Popeye and why a little elf? Why was Popeye beating him up so much and so often? I just didn't get it. But I'd wake up scared and upset every time.

Sometimes I'd wake up so upset and scared I was shaking and in tears, others, I'd be sweating. It was getting that bad.

I'd journal about the dreams. I spent all my free time trying to figure it out because the dreams wouldn't go away and they wouldn't leave me alone.

I had no one to talk it out with, so I kept meditating on finding the right person or group of people to do that, someone I could pour my heart out to and not be worried that they would think I was crazy. I needed someone to understand what I was going through.

At the time, I was going out with a woman, but I wouldn't risk telling her because I had already tried talking about it very lightly. I said something along the lines of, "Do you remember your dreams when you wake up in the morning?" She made some reply that let me know she didn't understand dreams and had no desire to learn. She thought dreams were some harmless garbage everyone has and said something along the lines of, "The dreams can't hurt you so what difference does it make? Don't worry about them."

So, I didn't waste my time trying to explain it all to her. If she was this uncaring you can ask me why I was with her. The answer is simple: the sex was fantastic. Hey, give me a break. I'm only human.

Remember I told you that as a bartender in Hollywood I was exposed to the entire human race, the good, the bad and the ugly?

I had to learn or figure out how to deal with the entire human element. And I had to figure out a way to do it without getting into a physical fight. Did I get into a physical fight once in a while? Of course. I learned quickly from experience that violence is the only language some people understand.

I am a nonviolent person by nature but I'm not stupid.

I could "feel" when a fight was going to happen and I knew I couldn't stop it. When I was in college I studied karate. I got up to a brown belt before I stopped. I would have continued to black belt but Life intervened and I had to stop taking classes. But I knew enough to be able to protect myself, which was what I needed.

But I also needed someone to talk out my feelings with. It got to the point where I didn't care if they understood or could help me. I just needed to talk it all out. By complete accident I found the perfect person and group of people to talk with.

I was going out with a woman and just like every couple, we were having. I remember one night at the bar a few guys asked me how I was doing. Now, I had always made it a point not to talk about myself at the bar. Work was work and I never forgot this was, above all else, a job. It paid my rent and bills and let me put food on the table. I didn't want my personal life talked about at work, because I didn't want to jeopardize my job in any way, shape, or form.

So, one night, near closing time, one of the regular customers asked me how I was doing. Since he'd had quite a few drinks and was feeling no pain, I opened up some and told him what was going on with my current girlfriend. I didn't go into a lot of detail … just some of the basics.

The next night he came in and I asked him if he remembered what we talked about the night before. He apologized and said he didn't.

What??? By total accident I'd found the perfect person and group of people to talk everything out with: my regulars who got too drunk to remember anything. Besides, they had their own problems they were running away from, so they had no reason to remember what we talked about. It was perfect!

I started talking with them when I knew they couldn't or wouldn't remember anything I said so I could be as open, as honest and as scared as I wanted and they wouldn't remember. Like I said, it was perfect.

Working as a bartender in Hollywood and dealing with all the people I encountered taught me how to be non-judgmental. I learned that if I passed judgment on them in any way, shape or form then they had every right to do the same to me.

I also learned if I passed judgment on them for any reason there would be friction. And it created an invisible wall between us. But when I became non-judgmental the friction and walls disappeared and we got along great. That's the secret I learned about how to deal with anyone, regardless of their age, physical appearance or background. It's how we all became friends.

Wow! I had friends that were White, Black, Mexican, Asian and American Indian. There were bikers, drug addicts, drug dealers, alcoholics, murderers, thieves, smugglers, prostitutes, pimps, multimillionaires, homeless people, actors, movie stars, musicians, successful rock groups, sex symbols and the entire human race.

There were some I didn't think were human, but I wasn't there to judge.

I only had two rules at the bar:

1) Everyone is welcome, but no one bothers anyone else.

2) No drugs.

Yeah, drugs were rampant but do them in the bathroom. Don't jeopardize my job by doing drugs out in the open at the bar.

My first rule told everyone they were safe in the bar when I was working. The women knew they were safe, so they came in all the time and had a good time. Guys for the most part go to a bar to meet or talk with women. So, if the women feel safe then the guys will follow and the bar will be a success.

When I was working behind the bar on Friday and Saturday night, the bar was always packed. Remember the cantina scene in the first Star Wars movie? That's what the bar looked like on Friday and Saturday nights. Rich, poor, big, small, tall, short, every race, creed and color. Gay, straight, and bisexual. Actors, movie stars, just to name a few. And I got along with all of them.

One bouncer was named Bear, and one was named Moose. So now I also had the L.A. Zoo working with me. Everybody fit in because no one fit in. It was fantastic. I loved working there.

Another true story.

One night I was working behind the bar on a slow evening. I was talking with three guys, who were not regulars. A guy came in wearing a dress, who sat seven barstools away from the three guys I was talking with. He wasn't looking for trouble. He just wanted to be left alone and he wasn't a drag queen. This was just a normal looking guy who came in wearing a dress instead of a pair of pants.

I went over and very nicely said, "Hi, what would you like?"

He very nicely replied, "I'd like a gin and tonic."

I said, "Okay." I made his drink, collected his money and returned his change.

Then I went back over to the three guys.

All of them were really disgusted by the guy in the dress.

One of them said, "You're SERVING that guy???"

I calmly said, "Yeah, why not?"

"Because he's wearing a DRESS!"

I looked at him and calmly said, "He has every right to be here just like you do. He's not bothering anyone."

This guy and his two friends were so disgusted they finished their drinks then and there, got up and collectively left.

I went over to the guy in the dress and sincerely said, "I'm sorry."

He very nicely said, "It's okay. It happens to me all the time."

We chatted for a minute and then some new customers came in and I had to serve them. He finished his drink and quietly left.

I'd learned the very valuable lesson of being non-judgmental.

Why does learning how to be non-judgmental matter?

It mattered because eventually I figured out that the same lessons about being non-judgmental that applied to all my customers in the bar also applied to dealing with and understanding my dreams. When that clicked then things started to fall into place.

I felt like the rooster that stayed awake all night waiting for the Sun to rise. Then suddenly it dawned on him.

I stopped passing judgment on what was going on in my dreams. Remember my recurring dream? I started talking with Popeye and the little elf. The elf built a chain link fence around him that Popeye couldn't get through.

So, the elf knew he was safe as long as he stayed out of Popeye's reach behind the fence. It was interesting to watch Popeye try to "con" the elf into coming over to him. The elf was too smart for that.

I didn't understand where the fence came from or why Popeye didn't just climb over it. When I talked with the elf I asked him where the fence came from. He said he just built it. I asked him how he did it. "Where did you get the fence?" He said he just created it like it was no big deal. I asked him to create another one while I watched. He asked me where I wanted it. I said, "Why not put it next to the fence you have?"

He said okay and the new fence just materialized in front of the other fence. I asked him if he could put the fence on the other side of the first fence. And instantly it was there. I asked him how he did that. He said he didn't know but it wasn't that hard. Wow.

Through dream control I forced Popeye to stop beating the elf up. I told the elf that Popeye wouldn't hurt him. He went over to Popeye and Popeye started beating the shit out of him again. Again, through dream control I forced Popeye to stop. He was pissed but he stopped.

Now what do I do? How do I do it?

I forced Popeye to let the elf hang out with him. Popeye bitched and complained the whole time, calling the elf completely useless, etc.

In one dream Popeye was the engineer of a long train on the tracks moving some kind of supplies from Point A to Point B. He was at the steering wheel. He was bossy. He made sure the elf knew he was tolerating him because he had no choice.

At one point the elf told Popeye that around the upcoming blind corner there was a large boulder on the tracks and if he didn't slow down and stop to remove it then it would wreck the train.

Popeye ignored him.

I forced Popeye to slow down. As the train slowly came around the blind corner there was a huge bolder that had fallen off the cliff, just as the elf had told him.

Popeye was stunned and in shock. Had the elf not told him that then the whole train would have been wrecked.

"How did you know that???" Popeye asked very slowly and respectfully.

The elf said, "I just knew." Like it was no big deal.

So, Popeye completely stopped the train and got out. Then he took a pick and started hacking the large bolder into more manageable pieces.

After a few minutes the elf asked Popeye if he wanted some help. Popeye just looked at him with a what-can-you-do look but Popeye did it with respect, not negatively.

So, the elf said, "Watch." And the huge bolder instantly disappeared.

Popeye was completely baffled and shocked. "How did you do that???" he asked with awe and respect.

The elf replied, "I don't know. I just do it."

That was it. Popeye got the message.

After that he became the elf's best friend and consulted him on everything. He even let the elf be the engineer while he stood right there and showed him how to do it. He guided him each step of the way like a loving father.

Sometimes the elf would sit on Popeye's shoulder while Popeye engineered the train. Popeye went from hating the elf to liking, then loving and respecting him.

He realized that somehow in ways he didn't understand, the elf knew things he flat out had no clue about and never would. He also realized he couldn't learn what the elf did or how he did it. He realized they made a good team because each one of them had strengths the other one didn't.

Then in the next few dreams the elf started to change. He turned into Peter Pan and would fly around sometimes.

Popeye sat there in awe. He and Peter Pan had become

very close friends, and Popeye would protect him whenever Popeye felt Peter needed it.

The bad dreams stopped.

One night while I was asleep and dreaming Peter Pan magically started to change into a real little boy. It wasn't all at once; it was a slow process. He'd change some and see how Popeye would react. He'd be that way for a few weeks and then he'd change some more.

Eventually he became a little boy completely. Popeye didn't care. He loved the elf who turned into Peter Pan who now was a real little boy with all the powers the elf and Peter Pan had.

One night the little boy looked right at me and said "Hi".

I was taken aback. It was the first time he acknowledged me or said anything. I very lovingly said "Hi" back. He started to talk with me more and more often.

After a few months I asked him what his name was. At first he wouldn't tell me and that was okay. One night he looked at me a little scared and said, "I'm Chris." I said, "Hi Chris." He smiled. When I woke up I wrote it all down in my journal, just like I always did.

One day, few weeks later, I was in the shower, and it hit me really hard: My first name is Chris, but remember, I killed him off a long time ago. I wondered if the Chris in my dreams was really a part of me. That night, I couldn't wait to get to sleep.

When I went to sleep, I saw Popeye and Chris. They were getting along great. I smiled at Chris. He smiled back. I very gently and lovingly asked him, "Where do I know you from?"

He looked at me and got nervous. He still smiled. Eventually he said, "Remember when you changed your name to Bryan and killed Chris off?"

I nervously said, "Yes."

He said, "That was me you tried to kill off. So, I just disappeared for a while."

Wow! I started to cry and cried so much I woke up. I wrote it all down in my dream journal and continued to cry. I was releasing so much and kept writing everything down: my feelings, the dream, everything.

The next night I saw Chris. I was scared and nervous because I had done everything I could think of to kill him off. I thought I was just changing my name, but I'd thrown everything connected to my past away when I left New York and moved to California. I didn't know Chris still existed as a part of me.

I very lovingly and sincerely said, "I'm sorry."

He said, "It's okay. I'm part of you. You can't kill me. No

matter what you do I'm still around. You may not see me or feel me but I'm always here."

I held my arms out and Chris slowly came over, looked at me closely, and we hugged. I wrapped my arms around him very lovingly and kept telling him I was sorry and that I loved him. He relaxed and calmed down. I asked him if we could be friends and he said yes. I had a very peaceful night's sleep after that.

It eventually occurred to me that I was able to force or order Popeye around, but I'd never talked with him before. I could talk with Chris now but, aside from bossing Popeye around, I hadn't started talking with Popeye yet. So, I also wrote all that down in my dream journal.

One day I started talking with Popeye, not ordering him around or forcing him to do anything because he was getting along really well with Chris and Chris loved Popeye so that major problem was solved.

I looked at Popeye and said, "Hi Popeye."

He looked at me the way Popeye does and said, "Hi" back.

Chris and I had become friends, so I asked Popeye if he wanted to be friends. He looked at Chris for support. That was a great sign as to how well they got along. Chris smiled at Popeye and nodded his head "yes". Popeye looked at me and said, "Yes, we can be friends." Chris took him by the hand and walked him over to me.

We shook hands. Then I woke up.

I wrote it all down in my dream journal. At this point, I felt I was making really good progress, butI still didn't know who Popeye was. I realized Chris was my inner child because Chris told me so. But who was Popeye?

When I was in junior college I read the book, "I'm okay, you're okay" by Tomas A. Harris, M.D. It was written in 1967. It's about the Inner Parent, Adult and Child inside all of us.

Doctor Harris worked closely with Eric Berne.

> *According to ChatGPT:*
>
> The concepts of the Inner Parent, Adult, and Child stem from Transactional Analysis (TA), a psychological theory developed by Eric Berne in the late 1950s. Berne introduced this framework to explain how individuals communicate and interact with each other.
>
> Key Concepts of Berne's Framework
>
> **Inner Parent**
> Represents the nurturing and critical aspects learned from parental figures.
>
> It can influence behavior positively or negatively, such as support or criticism.
>
> **Inner Adult**
> Acts as the rational, decision-making part of the personality.

Responsible for logical thinking and problem-solving.

Inner Child

Embodies the emotions, memories, and experiences of childhood.

Reflects the playful, innocent, and vulnerable aspects of an individual.

As I became friends with Chris, and then Popeye, I realized I needed to reread the book, so I did. It helped me a lot. I got my hands on every book I could that talked about the Inner Child. Several books started coming out. I read them all. Again, this was the 1980s. The internet didn't exist yet, so my progress was slow. I journaled everything and kept very detailed notes.

I noticed all these books talked about the Inner Child but none of them told you how to heal the Inner Child. They say be nice to your Inner Child and love your Inner Child.

Today, in the year 2026, a lot is written about your Inner Child but as far as I can see none of the authors effectively show you how to heal the Inner Child other than to treat them nicely and with love. Yes, that helps SOME. But it doesn't solve ALL of the problems the Inner Child faces.

Aside from reading books, I still had no one I could talk with about it all except the drunks in the bar at the end of the night. Mention the Inner Child to them near closing time and, as incoherent as they were, they would slur, "Oh yeah, I'll drink to that. Cheers!"

But in life you have to play the hand you're delt so I made the most of it as best I could.

So, Chris was my Inner Child. Who was Popeye??? Popeye and I were on speaking terms finally. He didn't resent me or dislike me. I was just someone who was talking with him.

One night in a dream I asked Popeye who he was. He told me he was my Inner Parent. That made sense to me now. He was always putting Chris down before the time Chris, as the elf, told him about the boulder on the tracks that was around the corner.

I realized somewhere in me was also an Inner Adult. I wondered when he would show up.

Eventually in one dream a new "person" appeared. To make a long story short, he turned out to be my Inner Adult. He was pretty beaten up, too. Through dream control I got the three of them getting along. That was nice, but something was still missing. It took me a couple of months to figure out what it was. I finally figured it out: All of the negativity and initial negative programming was still there.

Okay, now what? How do I get rid of all the negativity and negative programming inside my mind?

It took me over a year to figure it out because, again, no one was talking about these things.

One experiment after another, through trial and error, I slowly learned and figured out how to get rid of all of the negativity and all of the negative programming.

I kept careful notes on everything.

I slowly developed a process that worked. I used it on my Inner Parent, my Inner Adult and my Inner Child. It worked great but it left me feeling empty and hollow inside.

After a while I realized I wasn't going backwards anymore. But I wasn't going forward at all either. I was stuck in neutral.

So now what?

Slowly but surely, I figured out the problem was I had to replace the negative energy and negative programming with positive energy and positive programming.

My mental "Box" was empty of programming because most of it was negative and when I got rid of that I felt empty. There was some positive programming and some positive energy left inside, but not much.

I had no idea what to do.

Let me explain:

Everything you know or have learned is from observing the physical world with your five senses: Vision, hearing, taste, touch and smell.

Everyone can see the physical world. There's no argument and you don't have to provide proof: A chair is a chair is a chair. A rose by any other name is still a rose.

But with mental health, with self-help, with therapy, you're dealing with the nonphysical world and only one person can see it, the person going through the experience in their mind. And it's invisible to everyone else.

Your 5 Senses can't help you with the nonphysical world. That's what makes it so challenging. You have to learn how to see and hear with a different set of senses. It's a lot like how a blind or deaf person deals with the world.

Here's what I was dealing with:

I was finally in touch with my Inner Parent, Adult and Child. They finally stopped fighting with each other and got along.

But they were like the drunks at the bar: They were so beaten up and beaten down they didn't know how to solve their problems. So, they did nothing because they didn't know what to do. Nothing changed, nothing got better … and sometimes it got worse: Bad romantic relationships getting worse or ending, bad jobs getting worse or ending, etc.

Because they have poor mental health one of the biggest problems they face is they don't know how to protect themselves. So anyone in a position of control or power over them romantically, personally, or professionally can abuse it and they often do.

The drunks just drank their problems away. It was only a temporary band-aid but for them it was better than nothing because they never figured out the process of solving problems to their benefit or in their best interests. And their negative programming, programming they didn't know existed, kept them from doing anything.

Aside from learning how to do the basics in Life of putting a roof over their heads, clothes on their backs and food in their stomachs they didn't know much about how Life operated. And they didn't care. Those that wanted help didn't know where to go to find out. Their jobs were basically jobs where they traded time for money. They got paid by the hour, by the job, by commission or by salary. They're in a rut and they don't know how to get out of it because they didn't know there was a way out.

The drunks at the bar lived by the motto: Misery loves company.

I learned about my Inner Parent, Adult and Child. Then, I learned how to get them to stop fighting with each other. I figured out it was their negative programming and negativity that was holding them back.

I got them to stop beating each other up, but I hadn't figured out how to get them to stop beating themselves up.

Eventually I realized that when you beat yourself up, you're fighting a battle you cannot win. But how could I get them to stop?

Getting rid of the negative programming and negativity was a critical piece of the puzzle. I'd uncover some negative programming and negativity, remove it, readjust, take out some more, readjust, and so on.

Just when I thought all the negative programming and negativity was gone, I'd find some more. Then I'd remove it.

But I didn't know what to replace it with.

It took me several months to figure out a process that worked.

Eventually I reverse-engineered the process I used to get rid of all the negative programming and negativity and used it to put in all the positive programming and positive energy.

I didn't put the positive programming and positive energy in there all at once because I didn't know what I wanted, needed or desired in there. And I didn't know what would work.

So, putting in the positive programming, just like removing the negative programming, happened in Stages. I'd uncover some of what needed to be there, add it, readjust, add more, readjust, and so on. I kept detailed notes on all of it.

When I started to add positive programming and positive energy, that's when the real magic happened. Everything in my life started to get better.

The type of woman I was attracted to changed for the better. What I wanted from a girlfriend, friendships, a job and everything else in my life changed. Wow!

I finally figured it out and it was working.

How did I know it was working? Because all the abuse I was going through romantically, personally and professionally stopped. It didn't stop overnight, but it did happen slowly but it happened surely. It was a steady growth process.

I became calmer, more self-confident, more self-assured, more at peace. Things that used to bother me didn't anymore. I developed a positive outlook on life. I gained genuine self-confidence. I stayed away from negative people.

At the bar I learned how to put up an invisible protective shield protecting me from all the negative programming and negative energy in my customers. And because I was non-judgmental nothing bothered me.

Because I was gaining my mental health and I stopped

being judgmental I was able to see the Inner Parent/ Adult/Child in my customers. I could actually "feel" their negative programming and negativity. As a matter of fact, I couldn't miss it. It blew my mind.

I kept detailed notes in my daily journal and wrote everything down.

In gaining my mental health I figured the pieces out in Stages. Each Stage built on the preceding Stage. If I didn't complete Stage One, then I never could have figured out Stage Two because the processes I used to figure out Stage One showed me the beginning of how to deal with Stage Two. The processes I used to figure out Stage Two showed me the beginning of how to deal with Stage Three and so on.

I also learned the processes and tools I figured out in each Stage helped me in all future Stages.

When I first started to figure this out, I didn't know Stages existed. As I discovered the process I began to re- alize, understand and accept there were Stages and you had to do them in sequence. I learned this the hard way, by doing one test on myself at a time, keeping careful notes in my journal about what worked and what didn't. Eventually I figured out why some things worked and others didn't.

It's a lot like going to school. You have to learn the al- phabet first and understand what it means before you can read. If they put you in high school before you did the first grade then you wouldn't know how to read, write or do math. And high school would make no sense to you.

Anyway, using this method I slowly but surely figured the processes and Stages out.

Here is a rough outline of some of the Stages. It took me years to figure these out and how to resolve them.

When I didn't know what to do, I still had to figure out a way to do it with no one to talk it all out with except the drunks at the bar. Sometimes it took me months to figure out the processes for some of the Stages. Some Stages it took me a year or more. It was no fun.

Anyway, here are some of the Stages.

> **Stage One** was figuring out the root problem. Good luck with that because it was all invisible and my five senses (vision, etc.) couldn't help me.
>
> **Stage Two** was getting in touch with my Inner Child.
>
> **Stage Three** was getting in touch with my Inner Parent.
>
> **Stage Four** was getting in touch with my Inner Adult.
>
> **Stage Five** was accepting that they really existed even though I couldn't see them. I didn't know if I was uncovering something important, something that worked, or if I was going crazy.

Stage Six was getting them to stop fighting and beating each other up.

Stage Seven was getting them to stop beating themselves up.

Stage Eight was figuring out the problem was negative programming and negative energy.

Stage Nine was getting rid of the negative programming and negative energy in my Inner Child.

Stage Ten was getting rid of the negative programming and negative energy in my Inner Parent.

Stage Eleven was getting rid of the negative programming and negative energy in my Inner Adult.

Stage Twelve was figuring out the solution was putting in positive programming and positive energy.

Stage Thirteen was infusing my Inner Child with positive programming and positive energy.

Stage Fourteen was infusing my Inner Parent with positive programming and positive energy.

Stage Fifteen was infusing my Inner Adult with positive programming and positive energy.

And so the Stages continued.

As you can see, you need to learn the Stages in sequence and each Stage builds on the preceding Stage.

Try doing Stage Eight before you've done the seven previous Stages. Good luck with that. And if you get any of the Stages wrong then everything falls apart because they're all interlocking pieces. They all need each other and depend on each other.

You have to set up your Foundation Pieces first because without a strong foundation anything you build with eventually collapse.

How many Stages are there? It rounds off at around 40 Stages, and some Stages have multiple Levels.

My new friends asked me what I was doing and I was able to tell them. I told them in stages. I started by going into the shallow waters and explained it to them. I didn't jump into the deep end of the pool. I told them a little. If they came back with questions I answered them.

Then they asked me if I'd do the process with them. It never occurred to me to try it or do it on someone else. I thought I was the only person going through what I went through.

I started helping them. Much to my surprise it worked on them, too.

After a while and helping several men and women I realized we all walk down the same path gaining true mental health. Only the details are different.

I realized no one has had an ideal childhood. Or, if there were some people who did they were few and far between.

As each person I worked with got better, I saw them going down the exact same path I went down. Only the details were different. The process I figured out to get in touch with my Inner Parent, Adult and Child was the exact same process that worked for them. Again, only the details were different.

Then I used the process I figured out to get rid of all their negative programming and negativity and it worked beautifully. The process that took me years to figure out worked on them in a matter of weeks.

The same process I used to infuse positive programming and positive energy into myself worked for them, too. But it all got done in weeks, not months or years like it took me because now I knew what I was doing. There was no guesswork. I knew what to zero in on. And equally important, I knew HOW to zero in on it and HOW to fix it.

As I said, we all go down the same path, but the details are different. That's because not everyone had alcoholic parents, or drug addicted parents, or a father that sexually abused them, or beat them physically, and so on.

But the process, the blueprint I created for healing: that was the same for everyone.

Remember I told you as a bartender I learned how to deal with every aspect of the human race and that one of the biggest keys was to become non-judgmental?

When I was in Hollywood I was exposed to the best of the best and the worst of the worst, often in one night.

My customers were my teachers, and they didn't even know it. They taught me how to deal with anything and anyone. They were the cream of the crop. I was tested thoroughly and completely on being non-judgmental and learning how to deal with them.

The reason that was so critical to my figuring out how to get my mental health is because all the negative programming inside of me (and you and everyone else) was put there by other people.

You didn't just magically wake up one day with all the negative programming and negativity you have right now. You didn't just wake up one day and start beating yourself up for no reason.

It was put there one day at a time by your parents or whoever raised you. As a matter of fact, it was crammed down your throat. It just got reinforced as you got older and you didn't even know it was there. It controls everything about you.

As a child you are completely helpless and whatever an authority figure tells you automatically gets programmed into your subconscious mind. You don't even know it's happening because you're too young to understand it.

You can't fight back because you don't know how. They

are in complete control over you physically. They feed you, clothe you and they put a roof over your head.

Aside from needing food, clothing and a roof over your head, children only need two things: They need to be loved, and they need to be accepted.

Parents manipulate you by forcing their programming, their beliefs, and everything else on you, cramming it down your throat one day at a time. You can't resist because you don't know how to resist. And since they're your authority figures you just assume they're right and they know what they're talking about. Sometimes they do, others they don't. But you have no way of knowing or figuring that out yet, if ever.

Then puberty hits and you begin to question everything. But you don't know the negative programming and negative energy exists in you or where it is because it's invisible.

Even if you did know you wouldn't know what to do about it. It never occurs to you there's something better. So you don't even look.

You end up in personal, romantic, and professional relationships that are a reflection of your internal programming. You don't even know it and, even if you did, you wouldn't know what to do about it.

So it continues to control you.

One day, I decided to make my Internal Parent, Adult

and Child a Team. I had to figure out how to do it. It was working pretty well. But after a while I saw there were still problems. They still didn't feel complete yet.

So I decided to make them a Super Team because that's exactly what I needed: A Super Team whose sole purpose is to take care of me and protect me totally, completely and unconditionally under any and all circumstances and conditions. I had to figure out how to do that, too.

Creating a Super Team changed everything (again) for the better.

What image comes to your mind when you think of a Team? Then what image comes to your mind when you think of a Super Team? I think you'll agree a Team doesn't stand a chance against a Super Team.

Each member of my Super Team realized, understood and accepted that the State Motto for the State of Kentucky said it all so perfectly: "United we stand. Divided we fall."

It was through the men and women who asked me to show them what I learned and do it on them that I was able to polish and perfect the whole process. I had a template, a blueprint, and I saw it worked every single time.

That is how I gained true mental health and developed The Super Team™ Training.

At the beginning of my journey toward getting true

mental health, I was handed an invisible Notebook spiritually. It came to me in a dream.

There was a title written on the cover of the Notebook. It said, "The Proven Path to Gaining True Mental Health and How to Achieve It".

I was excited. All I had to do was follow the Notebook. I eagerly opened it.

It was completely blank except for one line at the top of the first page: As you learn these lessons be sure to write them down here and revise them as needed.

There were no directions, no instructions, no advice and no help.

To make it more challenging I was dealing with an invisible world.

How do you gauge progress? How do you gauge success or failure? What is a success? What is a failure? There was no template for me to follow. All I had was a blank page.

I got a physical notebook, then made it look like the one in my dream so I could write everything I learned down in it and I did. As I filled it up, I got a second one, then a third one and so on.

If I let you see my notebooks for the journey I went through, the processes I had to discover, and what had to be polished and perfected over the years through trial and error, the **Table of Contents** would look like this:

Table of Contents

The process of figuring this all out is a very long and lonely road. It's a lot like peeling an onion: The more you peel the onion the more the onion makes you cry. I kept notes on the whole process just like a scientist. This is where my training in College in Psychology and Sociology helped me a lot. My End Goal, even though I didn't know it at the time, was to make every part of my inner psyche a Super Team. It was very challenging.

You can't fake mental health any more than you can fake speaking a foreign language fluently. When you have mental health, no one can fool you into thinking that they have it too. You can see if they're lying.

So you have to ask yourself this critical Life changing question: How badly do I want true mental health?

The answer to that question determines where you will go in Life. It's a decision only you can make for yourself. It's also a decision you make every single day. You go at your own pace. You can stop and go as often as you want.

The lessons I learned in the physical world, like learning how to deal with anyone and being non-judgmental, applied to dealing with the invisible world.

This is how I learned how to gain true, lasting mental health.

This is the process I had to figure out one day at a time, one teardrop at a time.

There were times I was so depressed and upset I just wanted to end it all. Why didn't I just end it? Because ending it was a choice that had no time limit. I could do it anytime I wanted and no one could stop me.

This is where the lessons I learned from my Dad by going to Alcoholics Anonymous meetings with him later on saved my life. The AA Philosophy is: One Day At A Time. Easy Does It. First Things First.

Some days were so bad I couldn't take it one day at a time. I had to take it moment to moment. I'd be so scared and upset I didn't know what to do. I'd sit on my bed and shake I was so scared. Slowly, very slowly, I moved forward one moment at a time, one day at a time.

That's my story and how I figured this all out.

No matter what you're going through, no matter how bad it is, there is always a positive, healthy, constructive way out.

Before I leave you, I want to add some more of my notes.

Here is the **Target Card** Amelia told you I gave her at the beginning of this book on our first session:

> *I like, love, trust, accept, respect and protect myself totally, completely and unconditionally under any and all circumstances and conditions.*

If we worked together, I would give you that **Target Card** on our first session, too.

I would tell you to write it out longhand or print it out from your computer and put it on your bedroom wall. I want it to be the first thing you see in the morning and the last thing you see before you go to sleep.

I'd tell you to put another copy of it next to your bathroom mirror.

I'd also have you write a third copy, and I'd tell you to carry it with you all day long. I'd tell you to take it out and silently or quietly read it to yourself whenever you have a spare moment ... and I'd tell you to read it several times a day.

It took me several frustrating years of trial and error to figure out that simple Target Card. Please don't take it lightly, and please don't underestimate what it can do for you. If you take it seriously, it's going to change your life for the better.

Some more notes for you

I may be repeating myself here, but the lessons are so important, so valuable, that I'd rather repeat myself than leave them out by accident.

By being a bartender in Hollywood I got a crash course on the human race. I got my PhD in Street Smarts from the best University in the world: The School of Hard Knocks.

I'd like to show you the value of Street Smarts compared to Book Smarts with another true story: Two women came into the bar one night. It was getting busy but not too crowded. A guy started to cause problems four seats down from the two women but not connected to them.

I went over to the guy and told him point blank: "Shut the fuck up!!!"

He did.

I went back over to the two women.

One of them said, "I'm a psychologist. You handled that wrong."

I very nicely asked her, "What I should have done?"

She very firmly told me I should have gone over and said, "Straighten out. That's not how to behave in here."

The guy started acting up again. I looked at her and asked, "Would you like to handle this?"

She went over and very firmly said, "Straighten out. That's not how to behave in here."

The guy looked at her and spit in her face.

I did everything I could to not laugh.

She came over and sat down and wiped the spit off her face.

I calmly asked her how it went.

She said, "I've never been so insulted in my life."

She picked up her purse and marched out of the bar, never to return.

What she didn't know was one of the Key Rules in Life: You have to speak with people in a language they understand.

Being a bartender in Hollywood gave me complete exposure to the human race. I learned how to deal with anyone and everything. I sharpened my people skills by learning about people and their problems in the real world, not some textbook in college that tells you how things are supposed to be but aren't when the rubber hits the road. I learned a lot about myself, too. It was a real eye-opening experience.

Because I was a bartender, every single day people asked me for advice on their Life problems.

Because it was Hollywood I had the most unusual assortment of people dealing with every problem in the human spectrum. I dealt with and helped men and women of all ages, physical appearances and backgrounds. When they saw my advice helped and that I really cared word spread fast.

Hollywood gave me the best of the best and the worst of the worst. Often in one night. Some nights I learned the lessons easily. Other nights the lessons had to be crammed down my throat.

If I resisted the lesson enough then the same lesson was crammed down my throat several times until I finally got the message.

I viewed all of my customers as my teachers because they were. They didn't know that and it's okay. I knew it and that's what mattered. No matter what they threw at me I was grateful and viewed every one of them as my teacher.

Here are two of the very valuable Life Lessons I learned (There are a lot more but here are two):

   1) People spend their whole lives doing one

of two things: Pursuing pleasure or avoiding pain; sometimes they do them both at the same time.

2) When dealing with pain people always take the path of the least resistance, the path with the least amount of pain.

Learning how to deal with people in the real world taught me how to deal with all the bad programming inside of me because it was people who put that programing in me. Realizing, understanding and accepting this was a huge step forward for me.

I look at the years I struggled with this process, trying to figure true mental health out, what it was and how to get it. But now that I know what it is and have it, now I know how to do it, now that I have a process, I do it easily, naturally and effortlessly.

Before you know how to do something it's difficult but when you know how to do it then it becomes easy. It's just like learning how to ride a bicycle or drive a car. When I read my old journals where I was struggling with this I'm amazed as to how difficult it was then because now it's so easy.

The hard part was figuring this all out.

What stops people from gaining true mental health and solving their problems in a positive, healthy, constructive way?

1) Pain

2) Not knowing what the real problem is or how to resolve it or solve it in a positive, healthy, constructive way.

3) The work involved. There is no "quick fix"

4) Not knowing who they can trust or what works

5) Not knowing where to find someone who has already solved the problems they have

6) Not knowing how to gauge progress

7) Not knowing what constitutes proof

Just because someone has fancy letters after their name (PhD, etc.) doesn't automatically mean they can help you; and it doesn't automatically mean they can't.

Here's the real test: can they give you practical tools for true mental health and show you how to actually use them? If not, they're nothing more than a glorified, very expensive babysitter.

If you're not seeing real progress daily, weekly, and monthly, you're wasting your time. I don't care how many letters follow their name. If someone doesn't have mental health themselves, they can't teach it to you.

I'm not saying there aren't any therapists who *do* know what they're doing. I'm just trying to protect you from the quacks.

With true mental health you want help from someone

who's already achieved it, someone who's already walked down the road you're walking. Because they will know every roadblock, pothole, and problem you'll have. Just like when someone joins Alcoholics Anonymous, they want someone who has already walked the road they're walking.

In selecting someone to help you, don't fall into the dangerous trap of assuming that just because they have a PhD that they know what they're doing and can help you. Make sure you interview them. Ask them how long it will take before you start to see and feel results.

If they can't give you a straightforward answer, if they can't give you the tools to get true mental health and show you how to use them, or if they give you some nebulous bullshit answer, don't waste your valuable time and money with them.

With someone that knows what they're doing, how long should it take before you start seeing and feeling results?

My answer is a few weeks, tops. The people I work with see results during our first session and it gives them some badly needed hope that I understand what they're going through, why they're going through it and how to resolve it all in a positive, healthy, constructive way without drugs. They can see I've walked the path they're on.

My goal is to show them what's wrong, why it's wrong and how it got there. Then I give them the tools and show them how to use them. Then together we resolve everything. My goal is to put them in a position where they don't need me anymore because they can do it all themselves.

I've seen therapists that charge $166 an hour (and that's the low end of what they charge). They are nothing more than glorified babysitters whose clients make no progress. The therapists love it because you're paying their rent, week in, week out and you don't realize they can't help you because you don't know what to look for.

You can't fake true mental health. If the person you're going to for help doesn't have true mental health, then they can't possibly teach it to you. It's like going to someone who can't speak French and you think they're going to teach you how to speak it.

Want to find out how good your therapist is? Here's a simple test: If you have seen no improvement in yourself after three months, then you're wasting your time.

Another Life Lesson: You don't outgrow people. You outgrow the level they're on.

Everything around you, your job, friends, lovers, etc. is a reflection of your inner programming, for better or worse.

The same lessons I learned about dealing with people in the physical world applied to learning and doing Super Team™ training.

Some days I felt so terrified I couldn't even leave my bed.

But one painful, frustrating, heart-breaking day at a time I discovered that in gaining true mental health, Street Smarts beats Book Smarts every time.

You can't fake mental health. You either have it or you don't. It's that simple.

I'd like to leave you with a final thought:

Don't let the good things in Life rob you of the best things in Life.

Mental health is one of the best things in Life because it allows you to enjoy everything else and avoid all the negativity.

Mental health is worth whatever it costs. If someone offered me a billion dollars to go back to the way I was before I figured this all out, without hesitation I would look him straight in the eye and very firmly say, "No."

That's how valuable and priceless my mental health is to me.

Whichever path you choose, may Life be gentle with you.

Bryan Redfield

What's next for you?

That's the question you're asking yourself now. Whether you're a psychologist, a psychiatrist, a therapist, or just a normal person who is tired of feeling like you've been run over by an emotional freight train, one thing is certain: you're not alone.

You don't have to be struggling with multiple personalities the same way I was or nightmares the way Bryan was to still be experiencing an inexplicable mental anguish unlike anything you expected to feel in life.

What you do need to do is decide for yourself whether you're ready to become the person you were always meant to be.

It's frightening. Hell, sometimes it's downright terrifying.

I was afraid my heart would beat clear out of my chest when Amy took over my conscious body, moved my

Uncovering *Amy*

mouth, and spoke with her own weird voice through mine.

I have helped other people and watched Bryan work several times since then. It's the same with everyone: none of this works until you acknowledge and accept that the voice speaking through you IS you, just a different part of you that you could never see before.

Accepting that there's more than one YOU is the first step to healing all of them.

I have never met a therapist, psychologist, or psychiatrist who could offer someone the understanding, empathy, and help they truly needed because none of the people in those professions have gone through it themselves. It's noble of them to want to help, but all I hear from client after client is how their therapist or doctor didn't care about their problems and was unable to offer them any solutions that actually got results.

The solutions exist. You do not need to see a therapist for five years before you start seeing positive changes in your life. When you talk with someone who knows what they're doing, understands what you're going through, and has been in your mental shoes, the whole dynamic changes.

I consider myself healed now. I paid off my karma. I broke the chain by tending to my mental health. I didn't take revenge on my parents for the ways I was programmed. Instead, I simply walked away once I healed the damage. I picked myself up, dusted myself off, and walked away without trying to get even. That's how you break the chain.

I encourage you to take some of the steps from this book that we used to get started and try them for yourself. If your chest feels tight or you feel resistance to them, that's your old programming fighting for its life to stick around.

The key is that now you know you can change it.

If you think you're ready to experience a completely new version of you, there is contact information on the next few pages for us.

Thank you for reading this book. Every word inside is true.

Remember the next time you're struggling: this isn't all there is to life.

There is hope.

ABOUT THE AUTHORS

Bryan Redfield is a Dating and Relationship Coach with over 30 years of experience. He enjoys playing chess, exercising, and watching old movies. He teaches courses in how to find, meet, and date your ideal romantic partner. He teaches Super Team™ training for people he feels are serious. He can be found and contacted through his website, BryanRedfield.com

Scan to learn more about Bryan and the ***Super Team*** ™

Amelia South is a foraging instructor, practicing herbalist, and long-time wild-food cook who has spent over 18 years working with the plants of New England.

After healing her own gut and skin through real food and wild medicine, she began teaching others how to understand their bodies and the plants around them with clarity and confidence.

She's the creator of *Think Like an Herbalist*, a practical, no-BS approach to working with herbs that empowers people to become their own healers. Amelia loves teaching in person and consulting special clients on how to reprogram their subconscious minds with Super Team™ training to become the person they had always hoped to be, just like Bryan did for her. She enjoys hiking barefoot in the forest and drinking a nice hot cup of tea. You can find everything else about her at NoBSHerbalist.com

Uncovering *Amy*

If parts of this book felt familiar, unsettling, clarifying, or quietly validating—pay attention! That is your subconscious mind telling you there's something going on.

Did you finish this book *knowing* you have work to do and ready to start? Or do you need to take a little time to process and integrate what surfaced first?

Both responses are normal.

When you're ready to explore how the next steps might look—at your own pace—I've created a private page for readers who reach the end of this book and want more.

Learn more about how to create your
own *Super Team*™

Scan here

Want to stay connected?

Learn more about my work as an herbalist or follow along quietly: find me at

    Uncovering *Amy*

References

1 Note: I have since learned that while Dan was under the impression, like millions of other people, that this book was a story from a real person, that the story is fictitious and has a wildly controversial history. It does not depict an accurate representation of Aboriginal peoples and therefore I do not recommend you read it. The author is Marlo Morgan if you care to look it up.

2 Hatch, M. (2021, October 27). What does a white owl symbolize? Meaning & spiritual significance explained. YourTango. Retrieved August 13, 2025, from: https://www.yourtango.com/2021345551/what-does-white-owl-symbolize-meaning-spiritual-significance-explained.

3 Innes, LJ. The meaning of a coyote sighting. https://www.californiapsychics.com/blog/animal-sightings-symbolism/meaning-coyote-sighting.html

4 Anglis, J. (2024, August 31). What Is The Wendigo? Meet The Cannibalistic Cryptid Of Your Nightmares. AllThatsInteresting.com. Retrieved August 13, 2025, from https://allthatsinteresting.com/wendigo.

5 Joseph, B. (2017, February 16). A Definition of Smudging. Working Effectively with Indigenous Peoples® Blog. Indigenous Corporate Training Inc. Retrieved from ICTinc.ca.

6 Wikipedia. (n.d.). King Philip's War. In Wikipedia. Retrieved August 13, 2025, from https://en.wikipedia.org/wiki/King_Philip%27s_War

7 American Psychological Association. (n.d.). Schizophrenia. In APA topics. Retrieved August 13, 2025, from https://www.apa.org/topics/schizophrenia.

8 American Psychological Association. (n.d.). Dissociative identity disorder. In APA Dictionary of Psychology. Retrieved August 13, 2025, from https://dictionary.apa.org/split-personality

9 American Psychological Association. (n.d.). Split personality. In APA Dictionary of Psychology. Retrieved August 13, 2025, from https://dictionary.apa.org/dissociative-identity-disorder

10 Storms, S. (n.d.). Demon possession [Essay]. In The Gospel Coalition. Retrieved August 13, 2025, from https://www.thegospelcoalition.org/essay/demon-possession/

11 Harris, T. A. (1969). I'm OK, you're OK: A practical guide to transactional analysis. Harper & Row.

12 Maltz, Maxwell. *Psycho-Cybernetics: A New Way to Get More Living out of Life.* New York: Prentice-Hall, 1960. Copyright © 1960 by Prentice-Hall, Inc.

13 Janov, A. (1990). *The Primal Scream: Primal Therapy: The Cure for Neurosis.* Abacus.

Uncovering *Amy*